MY DAYS

R. K. NARAYAN was born in Madras, South India in 1906, and was educated there and at Maharaja's College in Mysore. He is perhaps most famous for his novels based in the fictional territory of Malgudi. These include his first novel, *Swami and Friends* (1935); *The Financial Expert* (1952); *The Vendor of Sweets* (1967) and *The Painter of Signs* (1976). *The Guide* (1958) won him the National Prize of the Indian Literary Academy. As well as four collections of short stories he has also published two travel books, two volumes of essays and three retold legends including *The Ramayana* and *The Mahabharata*. In 1980 he was awarded the A. C. Benson Medal by the Royal Society of Literature and in 1982 was made Honorary Member of the American Academy and Institute of Arts and Letters. He died in May 2001.

ALSO BY R. K. NARAYAN

R. K. NARAYAN

MY DAYS

A MEMOIR

PICADOR

First published 1973 by Viking, Penguin Putnam Inc., New York

This edition published 2001 by Picador
an imprint of Macmillan Publishers Ltd
25 Eccleston Place, London SW1W 9NF
Basingstoke and Oxford
Associated companies throughout the world
www.macmillan.com

ISBN 0 330 48443 5

A CIP catalogue record for this book is available from
the British Library.

Typeset by Intype, London Ltd
Printed and bound in Great Britain by
Mackays of Chatham plc, Chatham, Kent

FOREWORD BY JOHN UPDIKE

'Alive and Free from Employment'

The autobiography of a writer of fiction is generally superfluous, since he has already, in rearrangement and disguise, written out the material of his life many times. A novel like *The Man-Eater of Malgudi*, though its hero, Nataraj, and its author, Narayan, are not to be confused, tells us more about the India that R. K. Narayan inhabits, and more explicitly animates his opinion of what he sees, than his recent brief memoir, *My Days*. Not that Mr. Narayan's mischievous modesty does not lend an agreeable tone to this account of his rather uneventful life. Nor are his delightful gifts of caricature entirely inhibited by factuality. In *My Days*, as in his novels, one meets men so absorbed in self-interest that they become grotesque and emblematic: the young Narayan, seeking employment, grooms himself smartly to meet a prospective employer, who comes onto his veranda 'bare-bodied and glisten[ing] with an oil-coating, as he prepared himself for a massage; he blinked several times to make me out, as oil had dripped over his eyes and blurred his vision. . . All my best efforts at grooming were wasted, for I must have looked to him like a photograph taken with a shivering hand.' The man barks a rebuff of the boy, and then paces 'like a greasy bear in its cage.' This sense of imprisonment within character, of each person energetically if ruinously fulfilling his dharma – his vocation, a Christian might say – reached its peak in English fiction with Dickens, and perhaps requires a religious basis. In the liberal view, character is significantly malleable, whereas the traditional character-creators

v

fatalistically look into men for a fixed posture, an irrevocable passion. Narayan tells us that another uncle served as 'an inescapable model for me – his approach to other human beings, his aggressive talk wherever he went, his dash and recklessness . . . his abandon to alcohol in every form all through the day. (I portrayed him as Kailas, in *The Bachelor of Arts*, and he provided all the substance whenever I had to portray a drunken character.)' Few writers since Dickens can match the effect of colorful teeming that Narayan's fictional city of Malgudi conveys; its population is as sharply chiselled as a temple frieze, and as endless, with always, one feels, more characters around the corner.

Yet the creator's life, as described in *My Days*, begins in loneliness. A little boy, living with his grandmother and uncle, has only pets for company, and the pets all die. He goes to school, and hates it. 'On the first day I wept in fear. The sight of my classmates shook my nerves.' He cannot shape clay, and his slate is always smudged. Throughout his schooling, though he toughens into an athletic child of the streets, he remains difficult, intractable, uninspired. 'I was opposed to the system of being prescribed a set of books by an anonymous soulless body of textbook-prescribers, and of being stamped good or bad as a result of such studies . . . I liked to be free to read what I pleased and not be examined at all.' Taking his university entrance examinations, he flunks English – his best subject. And in the idle year this gives him, he begins to discover his own dharma – the vocation of a writer.

An aspect of this vocation, one feels after reading Mr. Narayan's fascinating middle chapters, is to have no other. His interviews for employment in business are humorous disasters; his enrollment as a teacher in the school where his father had been headmaster, a plausible route to respectability, is sabotaged by Narayan himself with the manic pugnacity of one of his own characters. His chapter describing the regimented foolishness of schoolteaching and his repeated escape from it approaches vehemence; the chapters following drop in emotional temperature, and trace a slow climb to success, contentment already achieved.

> That settled it. After the final and irrevocable stand I took [not to be a teacher], I felt lighter and happier. I did not encourage anyone to comment on my deed or involve myself in any discussion. I sensed that I was respected for it. At least there was an appreciation of the fact that I knew my mind. I went through my day in a businesslike manner, with a serious face. Soon after my morning coffee and bath I took my umbrella and started out for a walk. I needed the umbrella to protect my head from the sun. Sometimes I carried a pen and pad and sat down under the shade of a tree at the foot of Chamundi Hill and wrote. Some days I took out a cycle and rode ten miles along the Karapur Forest Road, sat on a wayside culvert, and wrote or brooded over life and literature, watching some peasant ploughing his field, with a canal flowing glitteringly in the sun. My needs were nil, I did not have plans, there was a delight in being just alive and free from employment.

It speaks well, I think, of the Indian society of the early Thirties that it allowed, after due resistance, this prospectless young man's rebellion against gainful employment; a contemporaneous American family might have driven such a child to France, or into bohemia – altogether out, in any case, of the home environment that has continuously nurtured Narayan's creativity. Madras, where he was raised, and Mysore, where he came to live, spontaneously fostered a fictional city: 'On a certain day in September, selected by my grandmother for its auspiciousness, I bought an exercise book and wrote the first line of a novel; as I sat in a room nibbling my pen and wondering what to write, Malgudi with its little railway station swam into view, all ready-made . . .' This novel, under the title of *Swami and Friends*, was finally published in England.

The literary London of Shaw and Wells, Conan Doyle and Wodehouse, the *Strand* and the *Mercury* had been brought, via magazines subscribed to by his father's school, into the center of Narayan's boyhood, and colonial India abounded in English-language journalism, though of a threadbare sort. (This reviewer once had the opportunity to ask Mr. Narayan if present, nationalist India, which has discouraged the teaching of English, would produce any more masters of the language like himself; his answer was affable but not affirmative.) In his first year of free-lance writing, Narayan earned nine rupees and twelve annas (about a dollar and a quarter); the second year, a short story sold for eighteen rupees; in the third, a children's tale brought thirty. He labored as the Mysore correspondent for the Madras *Justice*; Graham Greene became his champion in England, and found a fresh publisher for each of his earlier novels, which were critical successes merely. The author married, and his beloved wife's sudden death from typhoid, and his own slow recovery from sorrow via psychic communication with her, form the only significantly adverse incident in his gradual progress from journalistic piecework to international distinction, movie deals, and – crown of crowns – a travel grant from the Rockefeller Foundation. In prosperity and fame, his imagination seems to work as fluently as when Malgudi with its railway station swam into view: 'During my travels in America, the idea [of *The Guide*] crystallized in my mind. I stopped in Berkeley for three months, took a hotel room, and wrote my novel.'

Narayan's few revelations about his practice of writing heighten the value of this memoir. His desire to write in English was born of an early infatuation with English novels, beginning with Scott and Dickens ('I . . . loved his London and the queer personalities therein') and going on to the romanticism of Rider Haggard and Marie Corelli and Mrs. Henry Wood ('I looked for books that would leave me crushed at the end'). When he turned from mystical poems to his first novel, he let the incidents invent themselves: 'Each day as I sat down to write, I had no notion of what would be coming. All that I could be certain of was the central character.' The tale-teller, that is, is nearer the tale-hearer, in his openness to surprise, than college instructors of plot mechanics may know. 'The pure delight of watching a novel grow can never be duplicated by any other experience.' But Narayan's fertility would be tedious without his control and economy; he goes on to describe how his days of pure delight were followed by nights of 'corrections, revisions, and tightening up of sentences' so that a 'real, final version could emerge . . . between the original lines and then again in what developed in the jumble of rewritten lines.' His one confessed doctrinal resolve, as he set out, was 'to see if other subjects than love . . . could be written about. I wished to attack the tyranny of Love and see if Life could offer other values than the inevitable Man–Woman relationship to a writer.' The predominantly masculine interplay of his novels develops, one feels, from street life, from the skein of casual and passing conversation that he alludes to lovingly more than once. His days of journalistic news-gathering no doubt reinforced his habit of sociable curiosity, but the impulse perhaps dates back to the time when, an only child in his grandmother's house, he found it 'exciting, one day, to be asked to go with my uncle to the street of shops.' His days as a writer customarily began with a walk:

> All morning I wandered. At every turn I found a character fit to go into a story. While walking, ideas were conceived and developed, or sometimes lost through the interludes on the way. One could not traverse the main artery of Mysore,

Sayyaji Rao Road, without stopping every few steps to talk to a friend. Mysore is not only reminiscent of an old Greek city in its physical features, but the habits of its citizens are also very Hellenic. Vital issues, including philosophical and political analyses, were examined and settled by people (at least in those days) on the promenades of Mysore.

Narayan is one of a vanishing breed – the writer as citizen. His citizenship extends to calling up municipal officials about inadequate street lighting, to 'dashing off virulent letters to newspapers about corruption and inefficiency.' Such protests do not feel, as with so much American social consciousness, forced – a covert bid for power and self-justification. 'If I have to worry, it's about things outside me, mostly not concerning me.' What a wealth of material becomes accessible to a writer who can so simply proclaim a sense of community! We have writers willing to be mayor but not many excited to be citizens. We have writers as confessors, shackled to their personal lives, and writers as researchers, hanging their sheets of information from a bloodless story line. But of writers immersed in their material, and enabled to draw tales from a community of neighbors, Faulkner was our last great example. An instinctive, respectful identification with the people of one's locale comes hard now, in the menacing cities or disposable suburbs, yet without it a genuine belief in the significance of humanity, in humane significances, comes not at all.

JOHN UPDIKE, 1974

MY DAYS

When I sought confirmation on this point, my grandmother was horrified and said, 'What a fool to want to look like a monkey! You are in bad company. You must send away that creature. Wanting to look like a monkey when God has endowed you with such large eyes and all those curls falling down to your cheeks!' She was so fond of my curls that she never let a barber come near me, which meant that I had constantly to part the veil of hair with my fingers when I wished to look at anyone.

The peacock was not fully grown yet, but he bore his three-foot tail haughtily, and enjoyed the freedom of the house, pecking away every ant that had the ill luck to come within the range of his vision. Most afternoons, when I was tired of the sand dump, I moved to the threshold of the door opening on Purasawalkam High Road and watched the traffic, which consisted of cyclists and horse- or bullock-drawn carriages. A caravan of corporation carts passed along, stuffed to the brim with garbage, with the top layer blowing off in the high wind coming from the sea at this hour. The last few carriages forming the rear of the caravan were waggons, tar-painted and sealed, filled with night soil; the entire column moved westward and was soon lost in the dusty glare of the evening sun, but it left an odorous trail which made me jump up and rush in crying, 'Rubbish carts are passing.' This announcement was directed at Grandmother, who would thereby understand that it was time to begin her evening operations, namely, the watering of over fifty flower beds and pots. (She knew a potter who made special giant-size pots for her, a size I have never seen anywhere before or since, each one being capable of bearing a tree.) She reared in her garden over twenty hibiscus families, blue, grey, purple, double-row petals, and several kinds of jasmine, each scattering its special fragrance into the night air – numerous exotic flowers in all shapes and sizes. A corner of her garden was reserved for nurturing certain delicate plants which gasped for breath. She acquired geronia, geranium, lavender, and violet, which could flourish only at an altitude of three thousand feet in Bangalore, and stubbornly tried to cultivate them in the salty air of Madras. When the plants wilted she shed tears and cursed the Madras climate. Even after the plants had perished in their boxes, she tended them hopefully for a few days before throwing them over the wall, to be ultimately gathered into the corporation caravan going westward.

Filling up a bronze water-pot, a bucket, and a watering-can by turns, my grandmother transported water from a tap at the back yard impartially to all her plants, and finally through a brass syringe shot into the air a grand column of water which would descend like a gift from the heavens on the whole garden, dampening down the mud and stirring up an earthy smell (which tempted one to taste the mud), the foliage glittering in the sun like finely cut diamonds as water dripped off their edges. The peacock busily kept pace with us as we moved up and down bearing the water-pots. When a shower of water descended, the peacock fanned out its tail, parading its colours. At this moment, one could hear Rama rattle his chain, since he always felt uneasy when the peacock preened itself thus, and demonstrated his protest by clanking his chain and tumbling around on the roof of his own cabin. As the evening grew dim, I drove the peacock under a bamboo coop in a corner of the living-room. Rama would be fed with rice and driven into his cabin. He became purblind and bemused at dusk and one could push him hither and thither as one pleased.

Sometimes, when I sat at the street door, the peacock stood beside me. Every passer-by would stop to admire it; sometimes a youngster would beg for a feather to be plucked out and given to him. The first time I had this request I saw no reason why I should not oblige him; after all, he wanted only a feather while I had a whole bird to myself, and so I allowed him to pluck out a feather of his choice, just one. When he reached for it, the peacock stabbed the back of his hand with its beak and the boy fled screaming. I had not noticed till then how aggressive this bird could be. I began to notice that it possessed the temperament of a watch-dog. Quite a variety of persons had to pass in and out of our home all day, having business with my grandmother – mendicants, vegetable vendors, the tailor and goldsmith – and if anyone stepped in without warning they were viciously chased by the peacock. It generally perched on the wall over the door and directly descended on the visitors, pestering them until it was caught by its tail and dragged away.

My uncle, the only other member of the family, would not be home yet. He had a room upstairs which he used as his study and darkroom combined, where, when he was not washing the negatives, he pored over his class books. He went out in the mornings to catch the tram for his college and returned late in the evening. On holiday afternoons, he lugged out his camera on the tripod and fixed me in front of it. Sometimes he sat on the kitchen floor and narrated the day's events at his college; he was a member of the college drama group, and he explained to us Shakespeare's *Tempest* and how they were trying to produce it; he mimicked some of his friends who acted in it and that made us laugh; he was a good raconteur and I knew *The Tempest* long before I knew anything else. My uncle was Prospero and he described how his best chum, who did Caliban, entered his role so heartily that he proved a public menace during the rehearsals. He spoke of his professor, one Dr. Skinner, with great admiration, and we all admired him too, although by hearsay.

All sound ceased presently. The streets became silent but for the swear words emanating from the shop across the High Road while the owner berated his habitual debtors seeking further favours. He called his defaulting customers and their mothers names, and if I had picked up choice slang it must have been from the rich verbal arsenal that freely floated in the air.

Over all that hubbub one heard the tramcar grinding the rails at its terminus in the street of shops two furlongs away. Eastward of our home were shops and the tram terminus, where one boarded to get to the wide world and the sea-coast beyond, whereas the west side, where the corporation caravans went, seemed full of sinister possibilities. From that direction, one heard bickerings and curses and affrays from an unseen tavern. Corpses were borne in funeral processions in the same direction. I shuddered to look that way, but longed to see the shops and tramway at the other end.

*

It was exciting, one day, to be asked to go with my uncle to the street of shops. I clung to his arm and marched along. It was the evening hour again. I noticed a man with his hand and shoulder stuck through a bamboo ladder, going from post to post lighting the street lamps. The lamp-posts were few and far between: hexagonal glass shades on top of cast-iron fluted pillars. The lamplighter was an old man wearing a khaki coat and a blue turban, equipped with a ladder, a box of matches, rags, and a can of oil. He moved from pillar to pillar, unhurryingly. I was fascinated. I had never suspected that there could be so much to do to light up the dark nights. Clinging to my uncle's fingers, I watched him, my head turned back – a difficult operation, since my uncle dragged me along, never slackening his pace. The lamplighter went up his ladder, opened a little ventilator, took out the lamp, cleaned and wiped it with the rag, filled it with oil, lit up the wick and closed the shutter, climbed down, thrust his shoulder through the ladder again, and passed on to the next one. I had numerous questions welling up within me, all sorts of things I wished to know about the man – his name, where he came from, if he slept wearing the ladder, what he ate, and so forth; but before I could phrase them properly, I had to be moving along with my questions unuttered.

Other spectacles presently attracted my attention: the Pankaja Lodge, a sweet-meat shop with edibles heaped up in trays, presided over by a bespectacled man with a gleaming gold chain around his neck. The frying smell generated here reached me every afternoon while I sat at the street door of my home, with the peacock at my back, and made me very hungry. Today, my uncle stopped by to pick up a little packet of eatables for me, wrapped in a crackling brown leaf. I munched it, immediately forgetting the lamplighter. My uncle walked me onto the edge of the road in order to protect me from the traffic hazards of those days; one constantly heard reports of persons knocked down by cyclists. Milkmen with milking-cans in hand were driving their cows through the streets. I jumped aside at the sight of the cows, although my uncle tried to convince me they were harmless. When we passed an orange-coloured school building with a green gate, my uncle promised that I would in due course find myself there. I did not welcome the idea. It was a gaunt-looking building with a crucifix on its roof, and I hated it at first sight.

With time my outlook did not change. As far as this school was concerned, my first reaction seemed also to be the final one. In due course I became a pupil there. On the first day I wept in fear. The sight of my classmates shook my nerves. An old man with silvery stubble on his chin, turban crowning his head, clad in a striped coat without buttons and a white dhoti, a short cane permanently tucked under his arm, presided over the class of infants. Under his watchful eye we sat on the floor and kneaded small lumps of wet clay and shaped them into vegetables, fruits, and what not; we also cut out coloured sheets of paper and made more vegetables and fruits and also boats and quadrupeds. He brought his cane down violently on the table in order to gain our attention and tell us what to do next. I do not think I ever saw him lay his cane on anyone's back, but he flourished it and used it as a medium of self-expression, like a conductor's baton. My main ambition in life was to remain unnoticed by him. No matter how hard I tried, the clay never assumed proper shape in my hands. It never retained any symmetry or shape; while other boys produced marvellous imitations of all kinds of objects in creation, my own handiwork remained unclassifiable (perhaps I was ahead of my time as a sculptor). I was always afraid what the teacher might say; luckily for me I was a late admission and was given the last seat, and we were quite a crowd in the class; by the time he reached me, the time would be up, and we would have to run to the water-tap under the tree and clean up the mess on our fingers.

Thinking it over, I am unable to explain how this course helped me in becoming literate. If we were not kneading clay, we were only cutting papers and folding them. We were armed each with a pair of scissors; this was a welcome instrument in one's hand, no doubt, but the fingers ached with a dull pain at the joints when one had to cut out angular objects – the scissor points would not easily lend themselves to any manoeuvring around the corners. At the next stage I carried a slate, which displayed on its face a single alphabet or number traced over and over again, bloated and distorted by overlapping lines. This again was a mess, the slate having become white with the constant rubbing with the palm of my hand, as if a great quantity of talcum had been spilled on it, and it was always difficult to decipher the writing, which was white on a whiter background. Again my neighbours seemed to excel in this task; their letters were sharper, symmetrical, and they somehow managed to keep their slates shining black, against

9

which the white letters stood out clearly. The teacher did not seem to mind how I wrote or what I produced, so long as I remained within the classroom without making myself a nuisance in any way. All that he objected to, in me or anyone, was sticking out one's tongue while writing, which most children are apt to do. He kept a sharp lookout for tongues-out in the classroom, and tapped his desk violently with the cane and shouted, 'Hey, you brats, pull your tongues back,' and all of us obeyed him with a simultaneous clicking of our tongues – one golden chance, not to be missed, for making a little noise in an otherwise gloomy and silent atmosphere.

We were let off at four-thirty. Emerging from the school gate, we always ran into the rear-guard of the corporation caravan and followed it; there was no way of avoiding it, as its route and time were fixed inviolably like the motion of the stars in their orbits. Boys going in the same direction formed a group, and we chatted and played and giggled on our way home.

My grandmother examined my slate when I returned home, and remarked, 'They don't seem to teach you anything in your school.' Every day she commented thus and then ordered, 'Wash your feet and hands under the tap and come into the kitchen.' When I had accomplished these difficult tasks, she would have coffee and tiffin for me in the kitchen. She would have interrupted her gardening to attend to me, and resuming it, go on until late in the evening. From her gardening, after changing into dry clothes, and chewing betel-nut and leaf, she came straight for me. She would place an easy chair in the garden for herself and a stool beside it for me, fix up a lamp, and attempt to supplement with her coaching the inadequate education I got in the school. She taught me multiplication; I had to recite the tables up to twelve every day and then all the thirty letters of the Tamil alphabet, followed by Avvaiyar's* sayings. She also made me repeat a few Sanskrit slokas praising Saraswathi, the Goddess of Learning. And then she softly rendered a few classical melodies, whose Raga were to be quickly identified by me. If I fumbled she scolded me unreservedly but rewarded me with a coin if I proved diligent. She was methodical, noting in a small diary my daily lessons to be gone through. The schedule was inflexible and she would rise to give me my dinner only after I had completed it. I felt sleepy within a few minutes of starting my lessons; but she met the situation by keeping at hand a bowl of water and dabbing my eyes with cold water to keep me awake – very much like torturers reviving and refreshing their victims in order to continue the third degree. Grandmotherhood was a wrong vocation for her; she ought to have been a school inspectress. She had an absolute passion to teach and mould a young mind. In later years, after my uncle was married and had children, as they came of a teachable age she took charge of them one by one. She became more aggressive, too, as at teaching time she always kept beside her long broomsticks of coconut leaf-ribs, and whacked her pupils during the lesson; she made them sit at a measured distance from her, so that they might not be beyond her reach. Her brightest pupil was my cousin Janaki, now a grandmother, who at ten years of age was commended at all family gatherings for her recitations, songs, and prayers, but who had had to learn it all the hard way; she was a conscientious pupil and always picked up a choice of broomsticks along with her books whenever she went up for her lessons (an extension of the non-violence philosophy, by which you not only love your enemy but lend your active co-operation by arming him or her with the right stick).

*

* An ancient Tamil poetess.

Ours was a Lutheran Mission School — mostly for boarders who were Christian converts. The teachers were all converts, and, towards the few non-Christian students like me, they displayed a lot of hatred. Most of the Christian students also detested us. The scripture classes were mostly devoted to attacking and lampooning the Hindu gods, and violent abuses were heaped on idol-worshippers as a prelude to glorifying Jesus. Among the non-Christians in our class I was the only Brahmin boy, and received special attention; the whole class would turn in my direction when the teacher said that Brahmins claiming to be vegetarians ate fish and meat in secret, in a sneaky way, and were responsible for the soaring price of those commodities. In spite of the uneasy time during the lessons, the Biblical stories themselves enchanted me. Especially the Old Testament seemed to me full of fascinating characters — I loved the Rebeccas and Ruths one came across. When one or the other filled her pitcher from the well and poured water into the mouth of Lazarus or someone racked with thirst, I became thirsty too and longed for a draught of that crystal-clear, icy water. I stood up to be permitted to go out for a drink of water at the back-yard tap. When Jesus said, 'I shall make you fishers of men,' I felt embarrassed lest they should be reminded of fish and Brahmins again. I bowed my head apprehensively at such moments.

What I suffered in the class as a non-Christian was nothing compared to what a Christian missionary suffered when he came to preach at our street corner. If Christian salvation came out of suffering, here was one who must have attained it. A European missionary with a long beard, escorted by a group of Indian converts carrying violins and harmoniums, would station himself modestly at the junction between Vellala Street and Purasawalkam High Road. A gentle concert would begin unobtrusively. A few onlookers stopped by, the priest nodded to everyone in a friendly manner, casting a genial look around, while the musicians rendered a full-throated Biblical hymn over the babble of the street, with its hawkers' cries and the jutka-drivers' urging of their lean horses. Urchins sat down in the front row on the ground, and all sorts of men and women assembled. When the preacher was satisfied that he had gathered a good audience, he made a sign to the musicians to stop. His speech, breaking into the abrupt silence that ensued, was delivered in an absolutely literary Tamil, stiff and formal, culled out of a dictionary, as far away from normal speech as it could be. It was obvious that he had taken a lot of trouble to learn the local language so that he could communicate his message to the heathen masses successfully. But Tamil is a tongue-twister and a demanding language even for Indians from other provinces, the difficulty being that the phonetic value and the orthography are different, and it cannot be successfully uttered by mere learning; it has to be inherited by the ear. I am saying this to explain why the preacher was at first listened to with apparent attention, without any mishap to him. This seemed to encourage him to go on with greater fervour, flourishing his arms and raising his tone to a delirious pitch, his phrases punctuated with 'Amen' from his followers.

Suddenly, the audience woke up to the fact that the preacher was addressing them as 'sinners' ('*Pavigal*' in Tamil) and that he was calling our gods names. He was suggesting that they fling all the stone gods into the moss-covered green tanks in our temples, repent their sins, and seek baptism. For God would forgive all sinners and the Son of God would take on the load of their sins. When the public realized what he was saying, pandemonium broke out. People shouted, commanded him to shut up, moved in on his followers – who fled to save their limbs and instruments. The audience now rained mud and stone on the preacher and smothered him under bundles of wet green grass.

Actually, every evening a temporary grass market sprang up on this piece of ground for the benefit of jutka-drivers, and all through the evening hot exchanges went on over the price of each bundle, the grass-selling women shrieking at their customers and trying to match their ribaldry while transacting business. It was impolitic of the preacher to have chosen this spot, but he had his own reasons, apparently. Now people snatched up handfuls of grass and flung them on him, but his voice went on unceasingly through all the travail; lamps lit up by his assistants earlier were snatched away and smashed. The preacher, bedraggled and almost camouflaged with damp grass and water, went through his pro- gramme to the last minute as scheduled. Then he suddenly disappeared into the night. One would have thought that the man would never come again. But he did, exactly on the same day a week hence, at the next street corner.

The preacher was a foolhardy zealot to have chosen this par- ticular area, as this was one place where the second commandment was totally violated. If you drew a large circle with this spot as the centre, the circumference would enclose several temples where people thronged for worship every evening. Vellala Street itself, though a short stretch, had three temples on it – one for Ganesha, the elephant-faced god, next to it Krishna's temple, and farther off one for Ponni Amman, the goddess who was the frontier guardian at a time when this part of Madras was just a village. Where Vellala Street ended, Ponni Amman Street began, with its own row of shops and houses closely packed. If you went up Ponni Amman Street, you reached Lawdor's Gate (who was this Lawdor? What of the Gate? None in sight now), and it led on to Gangadeswarar Street, which again derived its name from the temple of Iswara (the Shiva who bears the River Ganga on his matted locks), a very large and ancient temple with a thirty-foot doorway, spacious corridors for circumambulation, and a tank for holy baths, public washing of clothes, and periodic drownings. (The tank still claims its quota of human life – one a year.) This temple of Iswara is really a focal point for weddings, funeral obsequies (at the tank), and spontaneous social gatherings, not to mention contact with God. The first nationalist agitation in Madras, in 1916, protesting against something named the Rowlatt Act, was organized here. A procession with patriotic songs and slogan-shouting started from the temple and went round the streets. I joined the procession entranced, and when we returned to the starting point, some enthusiast – the Pankaja Lodge, perhaps – provided refreshments for the tired crowd. When I went home after this patriotic endeavour, I was taken to task by my uncle, who was anti-political and did not want me to be misled. He condemned all rulers, governments, and administrative machinery as Satanic and saw no logic in seeking a change of rulers.

Beyond the temple at the street corner, there was a little shrine of Ganesha, which was once again a favourite of the school-going public; placed in a position of vantage, this god received a considerable amount of worship, as well as offerings of coconut and coins in the tin money-box fixed to the doorpost. Facing this was the temple of Hanuman, the God of Energy. All these temples attracted the citizens of the area almost every evening. Recently I revisited Purasawalkam and spent a couple of hours viewing the old landmarks, and I found, though multi-storey buildings and new shop fronts and modern villas and the traffic stream have altered the general outlook, that the four or five temples I have mentioned are still solid and unchanged, oil lamps still burning, and the congregations the same as they were half a century or more ago, surviving the street-corner Iconoclast as well as the anti-iconoclasts who sought to demolish him with mud and bundles of grass.

TWO

THIS IS NOT strictly coming in a sequence, for the following incident must have happened before I was put to school. I have already mentioned the temple of Ponni Amman. Once a year on a certain date the image of the goddess was taken out of its sanctum at the other end of Vellala Street and carried in a procession to our end of the street, and placed on a decorated pedestal at the entrance to a fuel shop opposite our house. I never understood how the fuel shop came to be connected with this festivity, but there it was – a hoary tradition by which it looked as if the goddess's annual vacation was spent at this spot, where all fuel business was suspended for ten days. The fuel merchant, of the name Kodandam, was a positive-minded character who would have fought out the issue if any change were suggested or if he were denied the privilege of playing host to the goddess. He was an expert in wielding and whirling a bamboo staff, so deftly that he could create a regular shield around himself and ward off any attack. He was a champion in this art, and brooked no performance of it by anyone else in his presence. He was a violent man who viewed it as a challenge to his own integrity, and beat up those who sought to display their proficiency. His shop, at the confluence of two roads, was the route for funeral processions passing westward; sometimes, when the body of an eminent personage was carried, pole-wielders marched in the procession as a special honour to the departed soul. It was an accepted convention that they should lower their staves and suspend their skill while passing the fuel shop. Otherwise there would be trouble. There were some unfortunate occasions when Kodandam blocked the funeral passage and beat up his challengers, and the pall-bearers fled, abandoning the corpse on its decorated bier in mid-street.

Such a man was the host of the goddess. He held his staff in hand and stood guard in front of the idol throughout the festival, and also gave a display of his skill from time to time. During this season our street corner was transformed. Flower-sellers, sweet-sellers, and toy-makers creating dolls out of pith and cardboard spread out their wares on the ground and lit up little oil lamps around them. I used to sit on the sill of a side window and watch this festival – tom-toms and pipes and trumpets creating a din night and day. Goats and hens were sacrificed at a mud altar in front of the image, late at night. And when Grandmother noticed a goat tethered to any lamp-post nearby, she closed all the wooden shutters, although I was dying to watch a proper sacrifice, in spite of my revulsion at the thought of it. But for this gory reminder, the festival was enjoyable and lively, and the image decked in a million flowers looked beautiful.

Turning back from my window, one evening, I noticed the fuel-shop man moving among the plants in our garden. I trembled at the sight of him, for I knew one of his activities was to bring under control the turbulent boys of our street. His services were in constant demand; he would go up and chastise the trouble-maker in his own territory and let go his hold only when the delinquent howled for mercy. When I saw him prowling in our garden, I had no doubt that he had come for me. Although I had done nothing to expect punishment, I felt he might attack me for the pleasure of it. He carried a basket in hand and had obtained my grandmother's permission to take flowers for his goddess in residence. Normally Granny would not let anyone touch the flowers in her garden, but Kodandam stood in a special category. (I learnt about this only later.) At the first sight of him I was filled with dread and at once fled upstairs noiselessly. From over the parapet I peeped out in the hope that he would have gone, but he was still there, prowling around, looking for me, perhaps. I quietly slipped into my uncle's study, hid myself behind some clothes heaped on a stand. I was satisfied that even if he came upstairs, he would not be able to locate me – although the smell of clothes waiting to be sent to the dhobi was suffocating. How right I was in selecting this concealment was proved an hour or two later when people began to search for me. As night fell, I was determined not to budge – it was terrifying, but I had to choose between the terror of darkness and the terror of walking into the arms of Kodandam. I was sure that Kodandam would wait for me indefinitely. Hours ago I had lost sight of my grandmother. I supposed she must be in the kitchen. But with Kodandam there, I had no courage to call her or go in search of her. My only means of escape seemed to be up the staircase. So I sat there still and silent even when my grandmother came up and stopped within an inch of me, calling my name aloud, and then my uncle, and then the three tenants who occupied the rear portions of our house, and their sons, all of whom kept shouting my name, without looking behind the clothes on the stand. I answered their call, but under my breath, 'I am here. Send away that man.' I watched them hold a brief conference.

'I went out and verified, but no one saw him at the fuel shop.'

'These are bad days – anything may happen, especially in a festival, child-lifters get busy.'

'Sometimes they carry them off for human sacrifice.' At which my grandmother wailed aloud. I sat stonily listening to this talk, but lacked the courage to come out of my hiding. They would chastise me for not revealing myself earlier. I was now as afraid of them as I had been of Kodandam. They went down, and a little later came up again in search of me, and then again and again. And every time they brushed past me, I was on the verge of shouting back, 'Yes, here I am; why don't you all go away? I'll come down when Kodandam is gone,' but I choked the words back.

Presently I heard a lot of commotion downstairs, various voices calling, mentioning my name, a babble over the drums and pipes from the goddess's camp. All sound in our house presently ceased. It became pitch dark. I was afraid to remain in that darkness any longer. I got up, softly went down the steps, and stood in front of my grandmother without a word as she sat in a corner of the house grief-stricken. She did not see me, a dim lamp was burning. I drew her attention to myself by declaring, 'I am hungry.' To her questioning, I gave no answer. I persisted in saying, 'I was only upstairs.' My uncle and the tenants and their sons returned late at night. 'We have reported to the police. They have warned all the railway stations by telegram, to watch for a boy with curly hair and only one pearl ear-ring.'

'Why only one?' someone asked unable to contain his curiosity.

'I always had only one,' I answered breezily.

'Nonsense,' cried my grandmother, 'I had both his ears pierced and fitted with such a fine pair of pearls set in gold! They were my father's when he was the dewan at Arcot. And this boy does not even remember it!' she said, looking at me accusingly. All of them turned to look at me, a delinquent who not only lost himself but also a great-grandfather's pearl; and they said in one voice, 'You must remove this too, as any thief may wrench it off with his ear.'

'And this chap will not notice it either!' someone added.

Though I am not certain, it was perhaps after the Kodandam incident that they put me to school, suddenly realizing that I was developing into an introvert dreamer with no knowledge of the outside world; they must have been mystified by my conduct, as I suppressed all my references to Kodandam the fuel-seller. I could have made a clean breast of it, but I had many misgivings. Perhaps it might recoil on my head. If they went and spoke to Kodandam about it, he might get ideas and turn his attention on me, or perhaps he had been stealing flowers and my betrayal might send my grandmother flying at him and that might bring further reactions in its wake. In childhood, fears and secrecies and furtive acts happen to be the natural state of life, adopted instinctively for survival in a world dominated by adults. As a result I believe a child is capable of practising greater cunning than a grown-up. When they failed to get the truth out of me, I was warned, 'Your name is now written down in every police station – take care!' I took care by turning in whenever I glimpsed the red turban of a policeman at the junction of Vellala Street and the High Road.

Nowadays, I had no peace of mind. Presently I lost the tranquil companionship of my monkey too. Rama was developing into a mischievous creature. By steady effort and trials, he had learnt to undo the waist-band and chain with which he was kept confined to his cabin.

On the first day he discovered his freedom, he took a leap up the roof of our house and leered at me from that height. I begged him to come down, but he did not care. He jumped on from roof to roof, wandered to his heart's content, and appeared on our tiles again late in the evening. He would not return to his cabin or allow anyone to approach him. At the slightest move on our side he would hop back and put himself just out of reach. If you tempted him with nuts and food, he would only eye them pensively but keep his distance. My uncle did his best to capture him, and gave up. 'Leave him alone,' he said. 'He is probably happier living on the roof-tiles. No harm can come to him.' The problem was not one of the monkey's own safety, but of the safety of others in the neighbourhood. He was not content to enjoy his freedom within the boundaries of our house but began to explore the city. He travelled up and down the street, all at a great height over roof-tops, and let himself in through any open window in any building. He picked up whatever he saw in a room and ran out when chased. Ultimately, he would return to our own house in the evening, wherever he might have spent the day, and occasionally gave us a chance to know what he had been up to. Once he brought home a black fountain pen, with its neck bitten off on the way, his mouth ink-stained. Another day he produced a shaving brush. He invaded the kitchen of a wedding party, filled his belly and the pouches at his cheeks with items spread for a feast, and needed no food for days to come. He ransacked methodically every fruit tree in the neighbourhood; people began to crowd at our door with complaints. We became unpopular. My grandmother declared, 'We can't help it. It's no longer ours.' The public did not accept her statement, and thought that in some mysterious way we were getting various gains through the monkey. At which Grandmother lost her temper and said, 'Why do you bother us? You may do what you like with that monkey, we don't care.' But they were helpless, the monkey was agile and elusive and could not be captured. My uncle, on a Saturday, when he had no college, spent the whole day cajoling Rama to come back. When everything else failed, he placed some food in a dish on an open terrace and sat for hours under the cover of a large blanket. When Rama edged cautiously near the food, my uncle shot out his hand, but Rama jumped back and did not appear again for a whole week – which time he seemed to have camped in the vicinity of a girls' school, snatching off whatever he noticed in a child's hand.

He had become notorious. The whole town was after him. I secretly prayed to all the gods I knew to protect him from his would-be captors. On someone's advice my uncle secured half a bottle of toddy from the tavern nearby, soaked some nuts in it, and left it in a mud pan on the parapet wall. Surprisingly enough, it worked. Rama at his next visit was stirred by curiosity. He approached the mud pan, picked up the toddy-soaked nuts and stuffed them into his mouth, and then stooped down and licked off the toddy remaining in the pan. After this treat, when he tried to move back to the roof-top, he found his legs wobbling; his gait became unsteady and he collapsed, unable to proceed farther. My uncle, who had spent the whole day organizing this trap, picked up the monkey and put him back in chains in his cabin. A few days passed thus and I resumed my dialogue with him from the sand pile. He had tasted the freedom of the roof and was evidently longing for it again. Like the magician Houdini he had become an expert snapper of bonds. He had slipped through his waist-band and was gone one morning. I never saw him again. I did not know whether he had been destroyed by his enemies or gone in search of new pastures or got assimilated in a herd supposed to be camping in a mango garden nearby.

Soon I had to adjust myself to the company of a mere peacock, who lacked the repose of a monkey (according to my notions), but was restless, always searching for insects and always wanting to be on the move, strutting along with his long tail (growing longer and heavier each day). He came up and sat faithfully at my side when I watched the street and tried to scare away our visitors. Soon he began to explore the outer space beyond Number One, Vellala Street. He would hop from our wall with an enormous flapping of his wings to the branch of a rain-tree in front of our door, and from there descend in a lump wherever he liked. He enjoyed his excursions and came back in the evenings by himself, or when one called out, 'Myla!' he would answer back with his long shrill cry from somewhere. We left him alone, as the neighbouring houses got used to his presence, schoolchildren admired him and fed him with nuts, and he got along with everyone except when they tried to pluck a feather from his tail. After I became a school-goer, I looked for him here and there while returning home and brought him back with me. He had begun to enlarge the area of his operations, and once he perched himself on the compound wall of our school – but when I noticed him there, with boys shouting around him, I let him be, never identifying myself with him, not being certain how our teachers would view it. Sometimes he would wander off in the other direction up to the toddy tavern, where happy drunkards gave him spiced nuts, which they generally munched while sitting around imbibing their drinks. Myla was always led back home by someone or other known to us. But one day two rickshaw pullers brought his carcass home and threw it in our garden.

'Someone seems to have broken his neck,' they said. He lay lifeless in the mud, with his broomlike tail stretching away.

My grandmother became hysterical at the sight of it and cried, 'Oh, take it away.'

They said, 'We thought you might want its tail – fan-makers will pay a good price for it.'

She averted her head and went in without a word, dragging me along. When she calmed down, she said to me, 'I always knew it would happen. They will eat it now. We should not have let it out.'

'If I didn't have to go to school, I might have guarded it,' I said.

A little mynah was my next pet. It had a brown body and yellow beak, and my uncle bargained it off a bird-seller in the street. I gave it pieces of bread soaked in coffee every evening when I came back from school. It was an easygoing bird, never inclined to fly away but moving within the house freely, fluttering around the rafters and coming down to perch on my shoulder when I returned from school. This particular species was supposed to be able to learn speech if properly taught, and I assailed its ear with a variety of sentences in Tamil for hours on end. It had remained safe in the living-room downstairs, but one evening I made the mistake of transporting it to the terrace upstairs. I placed it on the floor of the terrace, sat beside it, and enjoyed its pecking off of the bread crumbs from my hand. I had not noticed the cat on the roof a few yards away. At the appropriate moment, the cat swooped down and, clutching the bird in its jaws, went back to the roof-top. I cried, shouted, screamed, and swore at the cat. My uncle tried to comfort me with another pet in a few days – a green parrot in a cage which he suspended from the ceiling. My leisure hours were spent in standing on a stool and feeding it, through the bars, with banana, red chillies, or cooked rice, and attempting at the same time to make him repeat after me, 'Ranga, Ranga,' or 'Who's that?' I was hoarse repeating these, but the parrot never produced any speech – only nerve-shattering shrieking noises. Although we took every care to protect him, somehow a prowling cat seemed to have sprung to the flat roof of his cage, thrust his paws in through the bars, and dismantled his feathers. By dawn, mauled, disfigured, and bald, the parrot lay on the floor of the cage, unable to move, though still breathing. Someone came along who said he knew where damaged parrots could be repaired and rehabilitated, and carried it off with the cage, and that was the last we saw of the parrot, cage, and the helper.

My uncle somehow liked to have a pet in the house, to provide me company, perhaps, but he must have realized soon that we were not lucky with pets. He presently brought a kitten with a bushy tail (so different from that fierce mynah-snatching feline), who mewed when called – 'Nagu!' – sat with us at dinnertime, and enjoyed a small ball of rice mixed with ghee in our company.

I could forget all my previous losses now. A cat proves less bothersome than any other animal. In a few weeks, when it ventured out, a neighbour chased it down the street and it stumbled into the street drain, running in full flood, and was drowned.

Next was a little hairy puppy which was bought for one rupee from a butler serving in a European house beyond the tavern, who had assured us that it was a cocker-spaniel. It had enough of a coat to warrant this claim, but alas that creature too was presently lost. The puppy trotted about the house all day – as it seemed to me, in a state of perpetual hunger, snapping up and gobbling all kinds of articles: paper, rags, and cotton wicks which my grandmother lit for the gods, and also dry fallen leaves in the garden, manure, and sand, and lay on his back with a bloated stomach, struggling for breath, when I returned from school one evening. That was the end of the spaniel. My uncle made a resolve never to have a pet in the house again.

THREE

WHEN SUMMER CAME, the sun hit Madras with a ferocity that made people flee the city. Rich people went away to the hill stations like Kodaikanal and Ootacamund. For me the retreat would be where my parents lived. My father was the head-master of a government high school at Chennapatna in Mysore State which could be reached by a night's journey on one train to Bangalore, and then on by another one, a slow puffing train which passed through a rocky landscape. My grandmother gen-erally escorted me to Chennapatna when my school closed for summer, but she wasted nearly three weeks of my vacation in preparation for the trip. Her particular preoccupation at this time was the making of various sun-dried edibles out of rice and pulses, which would be fried and used as a side dish all through the year. She would also soak certain green legumes in salt water and sun-dry them for use out of season all through the year. All this was an elaborate ceremony, planned weeks ahead from February, when the air was a little damp. 'In about ten days after the Shiva Rathri festival, there will be no mist and I must get things ready,' she would say cataloguing several items of prep-aration. First, shopping for the spices and pulses. Fortunately we had a co-operative consumer store occupying a whole wing of our home, which we could reach by a side door beyond the bathroom. Actually our house was one big unit which my grandmother had partitioned and rented out to different offices and stores and families, keeping only a kitchen, living-room, and my uncle's upstairs room, for our own use. I did not realize at that time how much she depended on the rents for our survival.

My grandmother would select a quiet afternoon for visiting the store with her indent. When I returned home from school the floor would be strewn with gunny sacks and paper parcels. Somehow the sight of it filled me with delight. But when my uncle came home from college and noticed this activity, he frowned and made unpleasant comments, which upset my grandmother. She would retort hotly, and my uncle would say something more pointed in reply. I never made out what they said or argued about, although I watched and studied their faces keenly by turns, and tried to read a meaning. I only understood when she mentioned 'Gnana,' which was my mother's name. My grandmother would say, 'Can't go barehanded, I have to give Gnana something. She can't prepare anything herself; she is so sick and weak.' My uncle was a devoted brother to my mother and would not carry his objections further but, murmuring something vaguely, would disappear up the staircase.

My grandmother would soon have a battalion of helpers around the house, pounding and sifting and grinding and mixing and kneading on a large scale – her helpers were her friends, admirers, tenants, and paid servants. The house resounded with a variety of orchestration – the iron-clad pounder crushing, the swish of winnows, the ceaseless roar of the grinding stone, and the chatter of people over it all. Grandmother would have pulled out great rolls of palmyra mats and spread them out on the terrace. Differently shaped edibles would issue from little brass hand-pressers, and be set on the mats, and left there to dry in the blazing sun; she allotted the task by turns to the younger members of her following to watch with stick in hand for crows and to drive them off. When my turn came, I sat in a strip of shade all afternoon and scared away the crows by screaming at them, and was rewarded with an anna at the end of the day. Apart from the money, I rewarded myself, in the course of my watch, by peeling the half-dry stuff off the mat and eating it raw till I felt ill. My uncle ignored the turmoil in the house, averted his head, and preferred to make no comment whenever he passed the terrace; but my grandmother fried some of her product for him at the end of the day, and he relished it when I carried a plate to his room.

Eventually jars and containers would be filled and stored away for distribution at the appropriate time to various members of the family living far and near. My mother's share would be particularly heavy. 'Poor thing, so many child-births, so sickly, can't do a thing for herself,' my grandmother would keep saying to her friends. 'She needs more help than anyone else. She's helpless if I don't help.'

My grandmother's preoccupations were several and concerned a great many others. She was a key figure in the lives of many. She was versatile and helpful. She was also a match-maker; she pored over horoscopes and gave advice and used her influence to get marriages settled. I always picture her with a little spade or pruning shears in hand, for all her spare moments were spent in the garden. She could carry on discussions on vital matters with her friends while her hands were busy trimming off unwanted branches. Some days, mostly in the evening, someone would be brought in howling with pain from a scorpion bite. Granny would first tell the person to remain quiet; then she would go to the back yard and pluck the leaves of a weed growing on an untended wall, crush it between her fingers, squeeze its juice on the spot where the scorpion had stung, and then make the sufferer also chew the bitter leaves. If the victim made a wry face, she would remark, 'This leaf is *sanjeevini*, mentioned in the Ramayana. It can save you even from the venom of the darkest cobra. Don't make that face. Go on, swallow it.' Sometimes she consulted an exercise book in which she would have noted some special prescription for whooping cough or paralysis. When a neighbour came in a panic over a child having convulsions, she would drop whatever she was doing and hurry away, assuring the visitor again and again, 'Nothing to fear. Apply cold pack on the head and hot water at the feet; there will be no trouble unless you reverse the process.'

She had so much to do morning till night that it was difficult for her to disentangle herself from her activities and escort me to Chennapatna for my vacation. Hence my trip was constantly getting postponed, my grandmother always hoping that she would find some other traveller to escort me. But Chennapatna was a place which normally no one visited. No one had ever heard of it, although for my grandmother it was the most important place on earth, with her daughter and grandchildren living in it.

With my school closed, I had nothing much to do. All afternoon I wandered about the side streets with a gang of friends also at a loose end. I possessed an iron hoop which I rolled about the streets, followed by my gang, my route being up Vellala Street, turn left on Audiappa Mudali Street and then along Gangadeswarar and High Road – a large perimeter, which we travelled round and round, God knows how many miles in all, with the sun beating down full blast on our heads, barefoot, with dhotis tucked to the knee and loose shirts covering our backs. In our gang, one boy had a cycle rim, another one just a barrel band, and two more had nothing but just kept running with the group with their imaginary hoops rolling ahead. We were safe as long as we took care not to bump into cyclists, cows, or jutkas; we were the fastest objects on the road, and no one minded us. Most times we imagined ourselves to be a train (the automobile notion not having become quite so pervasive, and the aeroplane not being known), and ran blindly, aware only of the road in front and the sound of the running hoop in gravel. When darkness descended and the lamps in the streets and shops were lit, we dispersed to our homes – feeling tired, hungry, and ready to drop. It started all over again the next day. I practically lived in the streets in those days, and no one seemed to have noticed it until a postcard arrived from Chennapatna written by my mother, suggesting that I had better be packed off to Chennapatna at once as she was hearing reports from someone in Madras that I was endangering my health under the summer sun all day – the sort of sun which would 'shrivel up a serpent left on the ground.' My grandmother read the letter out to me and said, 'Play in the evenings, don't go out in the sun.' Of course she had no means of enforcing her rule, and the moment her back was turned, I ran out to the street, wondering why my mother was so ignorant as to think there could be snakes in our street.

Eventually, one night, we did find ourselves in the train to Bangalore, travelling in a crowded third-class carriage, surrounded by all the tins and baskets in which Grandmother carried the gifts for her daughter. We arrived in Chennapatna at noon next day, and immediately I was seized with a desire to return to Madras. The whole world looked so different now, new faces, new language, new voices. My parents' house was big, with a hall and courtyard, and my father had many servants wearing coats and turbans. The city itself looked mean and tiny. I missed my friends, the bare-bodied, rugged Madras boys. I missed my hoop. (My last-minute effort to include it in my travel baggage had been frustrated.) I clung to my grandmother, she being the only identifiable object in the strange land. The Chennapatna home had my parents, two sisters, and two brothers (the older one was Pattabhi, the younger one Seenu), and a baby; they eagerly received me and yet I found it an agony to be in their midst. I felt

30

shy and uncomfortable when my mother tried to converse with me, and nervous at the sight of my father – he looked forbidding and I was cowed by his tone, and by the spectacles through which he glared. In order to leave my mother free to nurse my younger sister, my grandmother, it seems, had taken me away to Madras when I was only two years old, and I could not think of any other place as my home.

All the children kept crowding around me, and everyone plied me with sweets and edibles. As evening came depression and homesickness became unbearable (the very shape of the brass lamps in Chennapatna made me sick); I wept unashamedly and demanded to be sent back to Madras.

It took me time to get adjusted to these surroundings, but gradually I began to enjoy the general pampering and the special food that my mother made for me. The servant carrying my younger brother in arms would escort us in the evening to the high-school compound, where we played; my elder brother would have his own engagement with his friends, and not mix with the children. He had a separate room in the house, where he kept all kinds of pets, and always locked up his room when he went out. Some days he took me with him and showed me various spots and introduced me to his acquaintances and favourite shopkeepers, who readily gave him whatever he asked for – a handful of sweets, fried nuts, puffed rice, and bananas, which he grandly passed on to me with a comment to the shopkeeper in Kannada which I did not yet understand. He would perhaps be saying that I was the fellow from Madras who had had a monkey of his own or that he would pay for the eatables later on. Another stop would be a cycle shop, where four bicycles were kept leaning against the wall, over a gutter. My brother declared to me, 'I can freely take any cycle here.'

'Do you know how to ride one?' I asked. In answer to my

query, he just took out one of the cycles and sounded the bell, and the shop-owner said something that again I did not understand, and my brother brought the cycle to the road, pushed it along a few yards, and then put it back in its place. We passed on to the school playground, where he joined a team of players and kicked a ball around, ordering me to stay behind the goalpost to admire his performance from a distance.

Some days later his cycle-shop friend got him into trouble with my father. One afternoon my brother had come home, gone directly into his room, and locked himself in. Shortly came the cycle-shop keeper, who had been all smiles the other day, now looking grim, propelling along with difficulty a cycle with damaged handle bars and awry wheels. He gesticulated and shouted wildly, and the commotion he created brought the entire family out, including my father, who came downstairs. My brother had taken a cycle on hire, had fallen off, damaged the machine, quietly put it back in its stand over the gutter, and come away without even paying the hire-charges. My father mollified the shopkeeper and sent him away, then knocked fiercely on my brother's door and got him out. His nose was blood-covered and full of scratches, his elbows were bleeding, and his clothes had blood marks and mud stains. My father glared angrily at him and demanded an explanation. He gave him a slap but before he could do further damage to him, the women screamed and rushed to his protection. My grandmother was particularly vociferous, and my father retreated to his sanctum upstairs, unwilling to have a confrontation with his mother-in-law.

This incident, which I watched from behind a pillar, frightened me out of my wits. I felt afraid of my father and decided to avoid his presence. As a person he had a commanding personality ('He has the personality of a commander-in-chief rather than a headmaster,' people used to remark), a stentorian voice, a sharp nose, and a lionlike posture – a man who didn't fuss about children openly, and never sat around and chatted with the members of the family as was the habit with others. He moved in fixed orbits at home. He had a well-worn route from his room to the dining or bathroom, set hours during which he could be seen at different points, and if one kept out of his way, as I thought then, one was safe for the rest of the day. He left for school on a bicycle, impeccably dressed in a tweed suit and tie and crowned with a snow-white turban, at about nine-thirty every morning, and he returned home at nine at night, having spent his time at the officers' club on the way, playing tennis and meeting his friends, who were mostly local government officials. At night a servant would go out with a lantern in order to light my father's path back home and to carry his tennis racquet, leaving him to walk back swinging his cane to keep off growling street dogs all along the path, which lay sunk in the dust.

When my father came home we stopped playing and shouting and became restrained. Having finished our dinner, we lay on a row of beds in the living-room carrying on some quiet game – such as enumerating, without looking, all the pictures on the wall. The enumeration started with 'God Vishnu on His Eagle' and ended with the sixteenth picture, entitled 'Vanity' – a woman decked in brocade sari and scintillating jewellery, the only non-god in the series. My mother's hobby was to decorate litho prints of gods and goddesses with gold lace and sequins and hang them on the walls. We conducted our sport in whispers and suppressed giggles as long as Father's voice was heard in the dining-hall. Mother always kept him company at dinner. He would describe to her his day at school, or criticize the food, or argue some point with considerable heat. Eventually, when we were sure that he was back in his room upstairs, we became riotous and flung about blankets and pillows. Mother, after putting the youngest one to

33

sleep upstairs and after seeing Father settled in his chair with his reading lamp and books (he read until after midnight), came down to give us each a tumbler of milk, and then sat down in the corridor for a while to converse with my grandmother (who would already be planning to leave me behind and return to Madras). From time to time Mother warned us, 'You must all sleep now, Father is reading. You will disturb him if you talk.'

*

It was my brother who taught me how to acquire and train grasshoppers. All afternoon we wandered on the outskirts of the town, peered into every ditch and culvert, stirred up the weeds and trapped the grasshoppers in little cannisters and brought them home; he always let me keep the green ones, and the large brown variety was reserved for his own pleasure. We kept them each in a cardboard box perforated for air, and stuffed in green leaves, sugar, and what not for their nourishment, and tried to teach them tricks, but invariably found them dead two mornings later. Although puzzled, we never wasted time in trying to unravel the mystery of their death, but sallied forth to collect fresh ones in the afternoon.

When the eight weeks of my vacation were over and I had to go back to Madras, I felt desolate. Having got used to the company of my brothers and sisters, to my mother's attention, and to servants, it would seem an impossibility to go back to the drab street companions, the abusive schoolmasters, the scrabby bench-mates from the Boarding, and above all the loneliness of the Madras home. But I had no choice. A postcard from that end in my uncle's clear-cut calligraphy intimated the date of my school's reopening and the fact that I was promoted to the next standard. (I have no doubt that I was pushed up by devious means, as the old school clerk who noted down passes and failures in the register was a constant visitor to our house and received many small favours from my uncle. Later he became my private tutor at home for many years and navigated me through the perilous seas of arithmetic and geography in particular, sometimes flourishing his cane as an aid to his teaching; occasionally he promised me solitary and starving confinement, in a cell supposed to be right under the crucifix atop the Lutheran Mission School; yet he was helpful at the time of promotions.)

My mother prepared several types of sweets to last me for weeks, and saw me off in the company of someone going to Madras. During my departure, my father hovered about to give me parting advice: 'Try not to become a Madras vagrant,' he said jocularly and gave me pocket money.

*

I remember being taken to Chennapatna unexpectedly again when Madras was bombarded from the sea by *Emden* in the First World War. Madrasis, not being used to any war since the days of Robert Clive, did not really realize that the city was being shelled from the sea. They noticed the searchlight beams sweeping the sky from the sea followed by explosions, and, watching from their terraces, wondered at the phenomenon of thunder and lightning with a sky full of stars. One shell hit the High Court building and shattered its compound wall; shrapnel were found in the Law College veranda next day; another shell hit the oil storage at the harbour and set it ablaze – a fire I could see from the roof of our house three or four miles away. The Crown Prince of Germany, commanding *Emden*, was roaming the high seas and sinking Allied ships, and while passing the Indian shores had shelled Madras just for amusement – without any serious feeling of hostility, perhaps, with the friendliest feeling at heart. Such is the complex stuff that warriors are made of; they destroy (or try to) for fun. It seems incredible that a commander of a battleship should come all the way, take all that trouble, to knock off a few feet of a High Court compound wall and set a tank of oil on fire. It scared the citizens who dwelt in the eastern part of the city – in George Town, nearer the coast – but left indifferent those who lived just a couple of miles in the interior. Many who lived in George Town harnessed their carriages and moved westward in the direction of Kilpauk. It was in keeping with an earlier move, when the sea was rough with cyclone and it was prophesied that the world would end that day, and many had their carriages harnessed and all valuables packed in readiness to drive off to Conjeevaram, forty miles away, the moment the sea should be noticed to rise and advance towards the city.

FOUR

WHEN MY THIRD BROTHER was three months old, my father was transferred from Chennapatna to a high school at a place called Hassan. He was advised by his friends to tell his departmental heads at Bangalore that his child was only three months old and could not yet be moved. But he was a disciplined officer and would not dream of asking for any special favour.

So for my next vacation, I had to go through a more complicated journey; an all-night trip up to Bangalore, a change of train for part of another night, a stop-over at a small station called Arisikere, a few hours of sleep on a desk in the waiting-room before joining a caravan of bullock-carts starting at dawn. At the proper time, I was awakened and put into a huge mat-covered waggon drawn by a pair of bullocks; I sat on a bed of straw covered over with a carpet; a stalwart peon from Hassan high school was seated beside the driver. Manja was his name. He was my sole escort from this point on (someone else travelling in this direction had brought me up to Arisikere from Madras). Manja kept talking in Kannada, which I had yet to pick up. He had a long moustache, and wore ear-rings, and chattered away with news of the Hassan home. Much of what he said was above my head, but he took a lot of trouble to explain in broken Tamil, 'The first thing you must promise me is to prostrate yourself at the feet of your parents the moment you see them. Otherwise I will never speak to you.' I didn't know why I should have cared whether he spoke to me or not, but somehow I felt intimidated, and vowed that I would prostrate myself at my parents' feet, although the notion was repulsive (as it still remains) that one should fall at the feet of another. But there was no contradicting him, as I was at his mercy completely.

Part of the way as we travelled along, Manja got off and walked ahead of the caravan, carrying a staff menacingly. Some spots in that jungle and mountain country were well-known retreats of highway robbers; one form of protection was to travel in a closely moving caravan with Manja waving a staff at the head of the column, uttering blood-curdling challenges. That was enough to keep off robbers in those days. We passed along miles and miles of tree-shaded highway, gigantic mango and blueberry trees and lantana shrubs in multicoloured bloom stretching away endlessly. A couple of times the bullocks were rested beside a pond or a well. The road wound up and down steep slopes – the sort of country I had never known before, for Hassan is actually a hill-station. (They continue to call it Poor Man's Ooty – Ooty being a hill-resort at a height of eight thousand feet to which government officials and affluent persons retreat in summer.) The over-powering smell of straw in the waggon and the slow pace of the bullocks with their bells jingling made me drowsy, although I was troubled at the back of my mind by Manja's injunction. It was a twenty-seven-mile ride. After hours of tossing on straw, we came to a bungalow set in a ten-acre field. Even before we turned into the gate Manja warned me to remember my vow. But the moment I was received into the fold at the trellised ivy-covered porch, I totally ignored Manja, and never looked in his direction, while he carried my baggage in. He never mentioned the matter again during my stay of three months; and I am certain that I would have shocked my parents if I had done anything so theatrical as prostrate myself on the floor.

*

My younger sister and brother were respectively seven and five – old enough now to be taken seriously by me. We played endlessly in the vast compound. The air was clear and a gold mohur tree in front was always in bloom. The house was of the colonial type, with arched doorways and high ceilings and venetian shutters. The trellised front porch was full of some purple winged flowers, constantly parachuting down. The gold mohur yielded enormous quantities of flowers. We plucked the long stamens out of each bud, hooked up their heads from opposite sides and tugged, and whosoever lost the head, lost a point. We could sit under the tree and play this game for hours.

My elder brother gave me his company whenever he could – but he was extremely busy, being involved in various sporting and athletic activities and in great demand among his friends; he spent most of his time outside our home and came in late every day through a gap in the lantana hedge, slipping into his room unobtrusively from a side door. He had to adopt this device since he was constantly admonished to return home before dark (an impossible condition for him). Hassan fields and roads swarmed with cobras, and the hedges were particularly dangerous, but he did not care. Once a tiger had escaped from a jungle and was seen here and there, and the town was in a panic; people shut the doors in the evenings, never venturing out after dusk. But my brother continued to come home at his own hour, bringing in fresh tales of the tiger's depredations – how someone was mauled here, a cow carried away there, and so forth. My father also continued his habit of club and tennis after school and never came home before nine in the evening. But he had the protection of Manja, who took a hurricane lantern and his bamboo staff to escort my father home safely. If there were more tigers and cobras to be feared, Manja only turned the wick of the lantern a little brighter and carried a heavier staff. As usual, we children were all in bed with blankets drawn to our chins before Father arrived, Hassan being so cold as to make my teeth chatter even in summer.

Some days my elder brother would take me out with him. We would go to a reddish, muddy pond to be reached from the back part of our vast compound, stand ankle-deep in the water, and fling stones to create ripples. Pieces of hollow reeds would come ashore riding on the ripples. I think we often risked being drowned when we sneaked out there, the only precaution my brother could take being a warning to me not to tell anyone at home. We needed a retreat like this because he brought cigarettes with him and we smoked. He had peppermints also at hand to cover our tobacco breath when we returned home. While smoking we were afraid of being seen by someone and denounced to the police, but this pond was a secure place; except for some insignificant young goatherd, no one came that way. We also smoked at home, under a zinc shed at the edge of our spacious compound. My brother used to tuck away the matches and cigarette packets under the eaves of that shed beyond the well. One afternoon my elder sister caught us red-handed, and we let her go after extracting a solemn promise that she would tell no one; we also gave her peppermints. But the moment she went in, she reported the matter to my mother, who later in the evening took me aside and asked, 'Is it true that you smoke cigarettes? Is this what you have learnt at Madras? I'm going to tell your father and he will, I am sure, take the skin off your back.' I had never been addressed so roughly by my mother at any time. I quailed and did not know what to say, but stood blinking stupidly until she said, 'Go and eat your dinner, you scamp. Where is the other fellow?'

My brother sensed the atmosphere and had somehow made himself scarce, and did not answer when called. For my part, I bolted down my dinner, went to bed, drew the blanket completely over my face, and lay still when I heard Manja's staff pounding the gravel outside. I expected, watching and waiting through the suffocating blanket, to hear Mother's denouncement of us and to have Father come swooping down on us, but nothing happened. I waited to be summoned, long after everyone had gone to bed and all sound had ceased, and only the night lamp was burning. But nothing happened; we had obviously been protected by Mother although betrayed by the sister.

*

Back to Madras. I had completed the final year at the Lutheran Mission School. The last group photo was taken after a farewell party, with our headmaster sitting in the middle, and the four teachers who were considered to be the cream of the teaching staff flanking him, a dozen or so of the classmates standing up in two rows behind. I have an old print of it – the one group photo which has not yellowed, browned, or dimmed with years, but remained remarkably fresh. It has a brilliance and glow which I find uncanny and embarrassing. It has stood up to the ravages of time, resisting every process of decay. The gloss and sepia tone are not a whit lost. Its freshness saves one from the natural depression that an old photograph provokes. Occasionally I try to amuse myself by recollecting the names of the figures in the photograph. Starting with the headmaster, in his perfect turban edged with a thin lace, and a silk coat buttoned up to his throat, an elegant moustache turned up at the corners with the utmost artistry – I never knew what his name was: one never thinks that a headmaster could have any other name. He was the perfect picture of a headmaster. He was a good man, soft-spoken, but rather inclined to using the cane at the slightest chance; he always prowled around with it in hand but had the good sense to put it away while sitting for the photo. He delivered a regular quota of cane cuts on my upturned palm on most Monday noons, in respect of absence from drill class on the preceding Friday evening. I skipped the class with reckless indifference; Monday the day of reckoning seeming far away and unreal. Six whacks on one's palm (with the choice of taking all the six on one or three on each palm) were less painful than the drill on Friday. On the right-hand side of the headmaster sat Guruswami, who taught us English, Tamil, and mathematics, and who tucked in a thick tuft of hair under a woollen cap, which was constantly popping up owing to the springy action of his tuft. I viewed him as a friend since he sent me on minor errands from the classroom, such as buying him *pan* or a packet of tiffin from the shops across the street, and I felt honoured by such assignments. His face was pock-marked and he was a homeless man, living in the school lumber-room off the upstairs verandah. The other teacher by his side was a soft buttery-faced man whose tuft stuck out of a short, felt headgear known as Christy's (London) cap. He was a mild, mumbling man who taught us history and geography, and was easygoing and more afraid of us than we were of him. He had the craziest name one could devise – Mrityunjayam – which we could neither spell nor pronounce. At the two rows of standing classmates I look hard and long but can't get their names except the one in embroidered cap over his tuft – what a lot of tufts in those days! – Kapali, our monitor, a supreme being, in my view, of dignity and authority. I hung upon his words and felt thrilled when he spoke to me. Where are they and how are they now? As if lost in a vast ocean. I can be sure of only myself in a black coat. (Which our tailor Appu Maistry took months to deliver. He came every month when the crescent moon was three days old, took a long look at the moon from our terrace, and then immediately gazed on my uncle's face for good luck. ' "If one's eyes fall on a virtuous face first thing after glancing at the new crescent, one will have good luck a whole month," say the shastras,' said Appu. Always in difficulty, he gazed on my uncle's face every month, for he was the only good man within his reach. He could have given me my coat – an old black one he had undertaken to alter – earlier if he had stuck to his machine instead of pursuing good men's faces. But he took months, compelling me to visit him every day. Still, he delivered it with every button stitched, in time for the group photo, where it remains enshrined for ever.) I cannot recollect a single other name in the photo, although for eight long years ours was a proud batch, reading, playing, and suffering our teachers together. When we came to the final year at school we held ourselves proudly aloof as became seniors, who occupied the rooms upstairs. We thumped up and down the wooden staircase heavily, authoritatively, as became the gentlemen of the school; stood looking down the parapet wall at the juniors swarming the school ground below, like Olympian gods eyeing fumbling and shuffling pygmies below. But I have to ask, Where are my fellow Olympians at this moment? Perhaps watching grandchildren, or waiting for their arrival from play or for a holiday. If and when through a freak of destiny there is a reunion of our group, I am sure we shall be comparing our lumbago, which keeps one pinned down to the *pyol* of the house, or the hyperacidity that corrodes one from within, converting food into poison, or the blood-pressure that jangles one's ear drums and decrees as in the case of Macbeth, 'Sleep no more.' All this speculation on the premise that they are all alive and recognizable. However, if I saw them now sitting in a row on a park-bench, I would pass them without recognition, as they might wonder in turn, 'Who is this hairless fellow striding along jauntily, unbecoming his years?' Very much in the strain of my American hotel manager, who told me once,

'Son of a gun, you must be as old as I am, though you don't look it; don't push yourself too hard, take care.' He had just recovered from a heart attack, and knew what he was talking about.

*

A change of school for the fourth form, to an institution called C.R.C. High School, an endowed school whose benefactor's name was too lengthy and was abbreviated for practical reasons. A school with no particular quality of good or evil about it, the chief interest in this change for me being that to reach the school I had to pass through the shopping area beyond the tram-terminus, which gave me a sense of enlarged horizons. School lessons became secondary at this stage – all kinds of other interests kept me absorbed. I became a scout, and proudly revelled in an exclusive world of parades in khaki shorts, double-pocket shirt, green turban, shoulder stripes, gaudy scarf, and a bamboo staff in hand; we saluted each other with the left hand, since it had to come from the heart, which is on the left side. Our great unseen God was Lord Baden-Powell, who had devised this institution in order to make the younger subjects of the British Empire healthy-minded, sturdy, and loyal to God, Crown, and Country. Our three fingers held up in salute were supposed to symbolize this triple loyalty to God, Crown, and Country. But alas, what a miscalculation! We were absorbed into the B.S.A. (Besant Scouts of India, Annie Besant being our President, championing the cause of Home Rule for India), and our three uplifted fingers indicated an oath to serve not God, Crown, and Country but God, Freedom, and India. The anthem we sang at the end of every drill to the tune of 'God Save the King' actually said, 'God save our Motherland, God save our noble land, God save our Ind.'

We were a very dedicated and purposeful troop that assembled in the compound of a home called Malabari House, for training

44

and drill under a scoutmaster. Performing at least one good turn a day was an inescapable duty for a scout. So we were given little good-turn notebooks in which to record the daily good turns made. It was hard to find any occasion for this fulfilment. I remember watching the street wistfully, hoping someone would stumble down or get run over so that I might rush to him and practise my First Aid (we were taught tourniquet-tying, and bandaging the skull, leaving the ears out). But alas, casualties were rare. I remember many a time jotting down in my notebook, 'Gave a coin to a beggar,' or 'Unrolled the mat for Granny to sleep on.' A scout started as a 'Tenderfoot,' and then was promoted to 'Second' and 'First Class' and given the appropriate badge for each class. I failed to attain the First Class badge, though I coveted it. I could never light a camp (or any) fire with just one match-stick; my knowledge of knots never went beyond the reef-knot, though there were four others to be mastered; and I could never read the signs and track a buried treasure. I always went astray. With all that, when Lord B.-P. visited Madras, I was one of those (ten thousand) who presented him arms with a bamboo staff.

After scouting, football became an addiction. We called our team 'Jumping Stars,' and kicked our football at a place called the Lake. (I don't know why; there was never a drop of water within miles of it; it is still called the Lake or the Spur Tank, though it is arid as a desert.) We were about ten – classed into goalkeeper, full-back, half-backs and centre forward – for each side, and we jealously guarded ourselves from being swamped by more; we had a captain called Jumbu. He collected four annas from each of us from time to time and financed the rest from his own funds. He wore the whitest dhoti and shirt and had the darkest face and hair; he tucked up his dhoti and always played centre forward and had an inborn sense of leadership. We all obeyed him blindly and looked to him to throw out marauders from rival teams, who would arrive earlier and try to take our ground at the Lake. Every day we met him at the corner of Subramanya Pillai Street. I could never guess where he lived, I never knew where he studied. He did not study at my school, but mentioned some unknown school in Saidapet – another world, in our view. God alone knew when he found the time to go to school and return home, as we always found him ready for the team at the street corner, wearing his whitest shirt and hugging a football inflated and ready to be played.

Our team was formed by Jumbu and we were from different schools. As soon as we were finished with school we gathered at the street corner and marched along to the Lake playground, lightly tossing, kicking, and passing the ball over the heads of pedestrians in the street or through the wheels of carriages, from one side of the street to another. People passed along unmindful of the nuisance. We went down Vellala Street, and across Ponni Amman Street and reached the Lake. At the field we had our ground beside the railway line. We rolled up stones to mark the goalposts, divided into sides, and kicked, passed, and dodged until darkness fell. Panting and perspiring and hungry, we turned homeward, retracing our steps; we paused at the street corner again to analyse the day's game and talk about plans for the morrow. We had problems to face sometimes, such as a challenge from a superior team, or fear of losing an evening game as the seams of the ball-cover were splitting at an awkward moment. But Jumbu handled all situations calmly. At the end of the year Jumping Stars did creditably, as out of the ten week-end matches on our records (at best our own composition, perhaps not verifiable) we had won ten – our only reward of victory being the lemons that were distributed, half per head, to quench the thirst; and even those were produced by Jumbu, we never knew how or from where.

FIVE

AFTER THE C.R.C., my uncle got me admitted to the Christian College High School, using his influence as an old student. I felt proud of my new school. I left home with a lunch pack early morning by tramçar to George Town, nearly four miles away, through crowds and traffic into the heart of the city. I had been suddenly let loose into a larger world. Purasawalkam, to which I returned in the evening, seemed a backwood. Christian College was practically the first building on the Esplanade, and beyond it was a road skirting the beach. From the college terrace one had a view of a blue sea and steamers on the skyline, and a salty air blew in all day. Our masters were well dressed, kind, and reasonable men, the students very different from the crowd I had known at the Lutheran Mission and the C.R.C. High School. Spacious corridors, a Gothic tower with a bell, a chapel, well-lit classrooms and halls, and an accessible library. At lunch-time, I carried my packet of rice and curd to a bookshop nearby and ate it behind the enormous shelves. It was one of the oldest bookshops in Madras, importing books from all parts of the world. I cannot explain why I was supposed to go there to eat my lunch, except that the proprietor was related to my uncle, who wanted to make sure that I ate my lunch in peace and privacy. After lunch, I browsed through the book-titles in the shelves until I heard the booming bell at the college tower. Some days, if there was a longer

47

recess, I crossed the road, hopped over the railings, and wandered through the enormous corridors of the High Court (the same place that had received a knock from *Emden* years before), making myself inconspicuous so that the sergeant who prowled around crying, 'Hush, silence, silence,' could have nothing against me. At the end of the day, I raced along with some of my class fellows to the Beach Station, clambered on an electric train, and got off at Egmore, the station nearest my home, saving thus the one-way tram-fare. I never bought a ticket for this journey, but on the advice of experienced friends, jumped off at Egmore and scampered through the coal-yard. I continued this practice until I bragged about it one day at home and was severely reprimanded by my uncle, who warned me that I might find myself in jail for this adventure.

*

The Christian College was, however, a short-lived glory. At the end of the first term, when we had Michaelmas holidays, I was sent off to Mysore, where my father was now transferred as the headmaster of Maharaja's Collegiate High School. ('Collegiate' meant that it had a university entrance class.) My father had no good impression of my earlier schools, was on the whole prejudiced against Madras schools, and decided to keep me in Mysore. Dr. Anderson, my headmaster at the Christian College, wrote him a personal appeal to send me back, and my uncle also pleaded with him to let me continue in a school where admission itself was an honour. But my father said, 'My school is good enough. Travelling every day in a tramcar is a risk, it is not safe . . .'

Thus ended one phase of my life as a man of Madras; I became a Mysorean thenceforth. At first, naturally, I missed the life at Madras – the companions, the streets and the noise, and above all the snobbish glow of belonging to the Christian College. But soon

I began to appreciate Mysore. It has an elevation of over two thousand feet and that makes the climate cool. Unlike Madras, where even a shirt on one's back proves irksome, here one could dress properly – coat, cap, and footwear, which my father insisted on both as a headmaster and as a father. The hilly roads of the city, seeming to go up and down, fascinated me, and the outline of Chamundi Hill illuminated at night had an air of shimmering mystery. The sky seemed to be more colourful and intimate, and the great number of trees all along the roads made passage to the school each day a delightful experience. I enjoyed the crowd at home too. I had now two more brothers to complete our family picture. My elder sister was married and had gone away to her husband's home at Coimbatore. My father himself seemed mellowed and ready to practise a philosophy of live and let live. His routine was the same as it had been elsewhere – school, club, and home; and he had now a much larger number of students and teachers to manage.

Soon I realized the advantage of studying in a school where one's father was headmaster. One got more people seeking one's friendship. The teachers were on the whole more gentle – except one troublesome botany teacher who fretted against the headmaster as well as his son, and who would go on saying: 'I don't care if someone is the headmaster's son. I'll throw him out if he doesn't come to class with coloured crayons.' It might be crayons one day or a slightly awry outline of a paripinnate leaf on my drawing sheet, or a blunt pencil or the snapping sound of a clipboard – anything that fifty others in our class might be guilty of. But the teacher focused his attention on me and would begin a long peroration on how he would deal with sons of headmasters. At that moment the whole class would turn in my direction and grin. But I had become less sensitive to such situations, and grinned back, which would infuriate the teacher further. He would

49

put aside the drooping plant in his hand and say firmly, 'I would not hesitate to send him out, even if he is headmaster's son. This is no laughing matter. Beware!' his eyes rolled in anger. I don't know how my father treated him officially – no means of verifying, as my father never discussed school matters at home. But my suspicion was that the botany teacher was no favourite of his. My father was as strict with the teachers as with the boys, and treated both alike. Voices were hushed when he passed by the Common Room. Still, a few teachers suppressed their resentment and got on with him, and were anxious that the headmaster's son should not disgrace himself through bad performance. Hence I was often advised by one or the other of them, 'If you have any doubts, come to me without hesitation.' Where was any room for doubts? Doubts arise only with at least partial understanding. If I could have had a definite notion of the measure of my ignorance, I could perhaps have specified the solutions as well. I used to feel embarrassed when such an offer was made, and I would say rather sheepishly, 'Never mind, sir,' or, 'It doesn't matter, sir . . .' Our zoology teacher was the one who persistently tried to improve my understanding; he would retort, 'What do you mean, it doesn't matter? It does matter. Don't you want to learn and pass?'

'I don't want to trouble you.'

He was a very short teacher, about four and a half feet tall. From a distance, one could easily mistake him for an overgrown baby but for his suit and turban. He sketched the anatomy of insects in so many colours that his fingers were always stained with chalk. Sometimes one side of his nose would also be streaked pink or green, and one could not help a smile while facing him, and he would smile back innocently. His initials were M.M. and we called him Millimeter. Unlike the botany teacher, this man was very cautious and never called me to account as the headmaster's son, but he had a persistent habit of cornering me in order to clear my doubts. We had practical zoology on Saturday mornings, and we were allowed to ply our scalpels on the carcass of some creature stretched on a board. I felt no doubt proud and important, like a surgeon in the making, and the scent of carbolic lotion was for us an exclusive perfume. I went through the motions of dissection with a lot of conceit, but with no intelligence whatever. I did what my neighbour did and came out of the class when the bell rang. And now there was no use questioning me about my 'doubts.' How could I tell the teacher, after he had lectured to us a whole morning, that I existed under a whole cloud of unknowing? My trouble was absolute abstraction from my surroundings. My mind was busy elsewhere – watching through the large windows the cows grazing the fields.

Next to religion, education was the most compulsive force in a family like ours. My outlook on education never fitted in with the accepted code at home. I instinctively rejected both education and examinations, with their unwarranted seriousness and esoteric suggestions. Since revolt was unpractical I went through it all without conviction, enthusiasm, or any sort of distinction. Going to school seemed to be a never-ending nuisance each day, to be borne because of my years. At Madras, in my Lutheran Mission days, my uncle was strict and would not allow me to stay home, however much I tried. When I lay in bed groaning with a real or feigned headache, he would merely say, 'Get up, get up. I'll myself take you to the school and speak to the teacher to treat you lightly.' At my father's school in Mysore, it became even harder – a headmaster's son faces a headmaster at school and a father at home. Though my father was generally uninterfering, he was addicted to watching the entries in the Attendance Register (the most unsightly volume in the world). Even in the classroom, where he was supposed to take an hour a week of English prose, he constantly paused during his lectures to snatch up the register and pick out the absentees between last week and this and demand an explanation. This was such a routine that he never got beyond the opening lines of a Lamb essay. ' "The elders with whom I was brought up were of a nature not likely to let slip a sacred observance, and ringing in the New Year . . ." ' At this point he would turn his attention on someone and demand, 'Sacred observance – can you explain what is a sacred observance? Oh you! Where were you last week? Urgent business, I suppose; let us see how much urgent business you generally have, from time to time. Get the register.' With a father and headmaster of this temperament, you were not likely to let slip a day. He would unhesitatingly make you stand up, and then declare the punishment, and, further, summon you to his room at home to say what a disgrace you were. So at high school, I maintained a hundred per cent attendance, although I had constantly to overcome the temptation to dawdle around a nearby nursery garden or a tiny lily pond outside, overshadowed by immense trees and studded with little brick monuments on its banks for the dear departed of a century ago. I resolutely absented myself from such felicities and got into my class with the first bell, otherwise the gates would be locked and late-comers shut out, until the headmaster arrived and let each one in with a proper admonition and warning.

*

Before actually entering the university for my B.A., I had a whole year's reprieve by failing in the university entrance examination held in the high school. I had expected to fare ill in physics and chemistry, both of which had defied my understanding. I never understood what I was expected to do with the 'data' provided with the so-called problems, the relevance of 'atmospheric pressure' or 'atomic weight,' or what to do with logarithm tables, or the why or how of a 'normal' solution. These points never became clear to me either through my own efforts or through our teacher's explanations. I had been certain of failure in these two subjects, but, as if by a miracle, I had somehow passed in them, though not with flying colours. On the contrary, I had failed where I was most confident – English. I failed so miserably and completely that everyone wondered if I was literate at all. My father, in spite of his strict attitudes in school matters, had one very pleasant quality – he never bothered about the examination results. He always displayed sympathy for a fallen candidate; he had no faith in the examination-system at all. But even he was forced to exclaim in surprise, 'Stupid fellow, you have failed in English! Why?' Proficiency in English being a social hall-mark, I remained silent without offering any explanation, though I knew why. One of our English texts was a grey-bound book of chilling dullness called *Explorations and Discoveries*, pages full of Mungo Park's expeditions and so forth. In my whole career I have not come across any book to match its unreadability. I had found it impossible, and totally abolished it from my universe, deciding to depend upon other questions in the examination from *Oliver Twist* or *Poetical Selections*. But I found in the examination hall that four out of six questions were based on *Explorations* – that horrible man the question-setter seemed to have been an abnormal explorationist. I gave up, left the examination hall in half an hour, and sat in contemplation on one of the brick monuments beside the lily pond.

My outlook on education has not really improved with the years. A few years ago when my daughter in exasperation threw up her studies, crying, 'Why should I bother about arithmetic?' I let her drop out without a word. Thereby she found more time at home for books and music. Now when my grandson shows any disinclination for school, I always support his cause, but of course his parents take a different view. As a grandfather I view his unseen masters as complicated, sinister beings who cannot be trusted.

SIX

AFTER FAILING IN the university entrance examination, I had a lot of time, since I could appear for the next year's examination without attending classes. That left me free for a whole year to read what I pleased, and ramble where I pleased. Every morning I left for a walk around Kukanahalli Tank, with a book in my pocket. It could be Palgrave's *Golden Treasury*, or Tagore's *Gitanjali*, or Keats in the World's Classics. After a walk around the tank, I sat down under a lone tree on a rise of the ground, opened the book, and partially read and partially observed the water birds diving in. Of course cows and goats, ubiquitous in Mysore, grazed around. But everything fitted into the scheme beautifully. I read until noon and started back home. I do not know if it was wise of them to have failed me and let me loose for a whole year and thus spoil me. Sometimes I went back to the Kukanahalli Tank in the late afternoon, when the evening sun touched the rippling water-surface to produce uncanny lighting effects, and the western sky presented a gorgeous display of colours and cloud formations at sunset. Even today, I would assert, after having visited many parts of the world, that nowhere can you witness such masterpiece sunsets as in Mysore. I would sit on a bench on the tank and watch the sun's performance, the gradual fading of the colours in the sky, and the emergence of the first single star at dusk. When the monsoon broke, one could watch dark mountainous clouds mustering, edged with lightning; these would develop awesome pyrotechnics. In June, drizzle and sunshine alternating, leaving gold mohur, flame of the forests, and jacaranda in bloom along the avenues. In July and August the never-ending downpour, grey leaden skies, and the damp air blowing. I was fascinated by all the seasonal changes. Tagore's poetry (although I may be somewhat more critical today) swept me off my feet in those days. When I read:

> In the deep shadows of the rainy July,
> with secret steps, thou walkest.

I felt I was inducted into the secrets of Nature's Glory. So did much of Palgrave, Keats, Shelley, Byron, and Browning. They spoke of an experience that was real and immediate in my surroundings, and stirred in me a deep response. Perhaps I was in an extremely raw state of mind. My failure at the examination, and seeing my classmates marching ahead, induced a mood of pessimism and martyrdom which, in some strange manner, seemed to have deepened my sensibilities.

I enjoyed every moment of living in Mysore. Sometimes I loitered through the parks and the illuminated vicinities of the Maharaja's Palace. Some days I climbed the thousand steps of the hill and prayed at the shrine of Chamundi, made coconut offerings, and ate them with great relish on the way back. Some days I would notice the gathering storm and flee before it, running down the thousand steps and a couple of miles from the foot of the hill, to reach home drenched, dripping, and panting, but feeling victorious at having survived the blinding lightning and thunder. In some of these enterprises I would have the company of my younger brother Seenu and a few friends. Chamundi Hill offered not only a temple to visit, but also uncharted slopes, boulders, creeks, and unsuspected retreats. Our exploration once brought us to a cave-temple with pillared platforms, secret chambers, and underground cellars, the entire structure roofed over by a huge rock, now deserted and concealed under wild, thorny vegetation, at the southern base of Chamundi Hill. I took to visiting this cave regularly, not caring for the rumour that the place might be harbouring reptiles and cheetahs in its cellars. We went down, tempting providence, to the bottom-most levels, and inscribed our names and addresses on the stone walls with fragments of charcoal which we found strewn about. We braved it, feeling all the while that we were walking into the jaws of death just to inscribe our names on the walls. At the other extreme, my name could also be found at the highest point of Mysore – the topmost chamber of the tower of the Chamundi Temple, which I once reached by a series of ladders to find myself standing on the gigantic lolling tongue of a gargoyle decorating the tower. The view of Mysore City from this height was breath-taking, and I retraced the steps after inscribing my name and address on the wall with the message 'Past is gone, present is fleeting, future is vague.' I think my name with the message must still be there, if the renovators have not reached that height or the depth of the cave-cellars in Chamundi Hill. I am not so sure of the latter. A couple of years ago, I tried to revisit the cave and found the place tidied up and occupied. A barbed-wire fence encircled it, the ground around cemented, potted plants kept in rows, electric lights and waterpumps for the garden; the entire cave structure was lime-washed, cleared up, and made fit for a royal residence. A member of the royal family seemed to have taken a fancy to this spot, unfortunately, and cleared it and kept off the public with an armed guard at the gate, not realizing that it's a sacred duty of every enlightened citizen to leave a perfect ruin alone. A ruin is not achieved in a day; it's a result of a long maturing process; unhampered vegetation, thorns, brambles, reptiles, wild beasts, fauna, flora, weather, mud, and all the elements have to combine to create a perfect ruin. I would view any improvement on this an act of vandalism. Royalty keep off, I'd say.

*

Being the headmaster's son, I had extraordinary privileges in the school library. During summer vacation the library clerk threw open the shelves at all hours, on all days, although he made it nearly impossible with his rules and his form-filling for an ordinary student to take any book home. He thought, perhaps, that he would earn a word of commendation from the headmaster for the privilege shown to his son, although I doubt if my father would have approved of any special treatment for us (my elder brother also obtained these facilities). On holidays, I spent the afternoons at the library, read all the magazines on the table, and had all the shelves opened. I took out four books at a time and read them through at a stretch. A passage in one of our textbooks from Scott's *The Bride of Lammermoor* had whetted my taste for the mists of the Highlands and the drama and romance occurring in that haze. I read *The Bride of Lammermoor* and six other novels by Sir Walter, and relished the strong doses of love and hate that agitated the Highland clans. I admired Scott so much that I searched for his portrait and found one in a second-hand bookshop – a copper engraving as a frontispiece to a double-column edition in microscopic type, containing three novels in one volume, with many illustrations that brought to life all those strong-willed men and forlorn women in their castle homes. After Scott I picked up a whole row of Dickens and loved his London and the queer personalities therein. Rider Haggard, Marie Corelli, Molière and Pope and Marlowe, Tolstoi, Thomas Hardy – an indiscriminate jumble; I read everything with the utmost enjoyment.

I and my elder brother shared a room outside the main house

but in the same compound, and there we competed with each other in reading. He read fast, noted in a diary his impressions of a book, and copied down passages that appealed to him. Sometimes, he read aloud a play – Shakespeare or Molière – and compelled me to set aside my own book and listen to his reading. For days on end we stayed at home and read, hardly aware of the seasons or the time passing. At eating time we would make a dash into the main house in which my parents and brothers lived, and return by the back door to our room to resume our reading. We were in a world of our own. In addition to fiction, part of the time I enjoyed reading the history of English literature. A minor work on this, Long's *English Literature*, fell into my hands and I found it interesting right from the facsimile of Magna Carta in the frontispiece. It became my ambition in life to read at least two books from each literary period, starting with the Anglo-Normans. But it didn't work. Although Long's summaries of early literature were fascinating, I realized that the actual work in each case was unreadable. *Beowulf* I found baffling. Spenser confounded me. I could only begin from Ben Jonson, and allotted an hour a day for a methodical study of English literature. I imposed on myself a profound discipline and went through it heroically. At the end of sixty minutes, I returned to fiction with relief.

I loved tragic endings in novels. I looked for books that would leave me crushed at the end. Thus Mrs. Henry Wood's *East Lynne* left me shedding bitter tears, and I read it again and again. The heroine, the lady of a well-to-do family, committed adultery, ran away, was deserted by the seducer, was left for dead in a railway accident, but surviving it came to work as a menial in her own home, and looked after the children. Of course, she was not recognizable, her chief means of disguise being a pair of blue spectacles, so that her children and husband treated her as a servant throughout; when she was dying of 'consumption' and coughing her misguided life out, she revealed herself in a harrowing manner. Reading and rereading it always produced a lump in my throat, and that was the most luxurious sadness you could think of. I deliberately looked for stories in which the heroine wasted away in consumption (unless it was the sort of end that befell a lovely woman stooping to folly and finding too late that men betray). I found a lot of it in Dickens, but the most satisfying book in this category was *Passionate Friends* by H. G. Wells (though I cannot recollect if 'consumption' ended the heroine's career, or strychnine). One book which I discovered with a whoop of joy was by Victoria Cross (Who was this? Never came across a second book by this author), in which the good lady dies of plague or cholera, leaving the man who loved her shattered and benumbed with grief for the rest of his life. Marie Corelli appealed to me most. I have recently tried to reread some of her books without much success, although one could still accept the synthetic atmosphere she could create of Norway, Egypt, or the English countryside. In a state of juvenile innocence, the mind absorbs the essence through all the dross. But at that stage of my literary searching I read about a dozen of her novels, and felt a regret at the end of each book that it was not longer than five hundred pages! Her overcharged romanticism and her pungent asides about English society and literary critics filled me with admiration. I cut out a portrait of her from *Bookman* and mounted it on my bookshelf.

My father utilized to the utmost all the library budget and any balance left over from other departments such as sports; the result was that the high-school reading-room had on its table magazines from every part of the world. Week-ends, when foreign mail arrived, were an exciting time. Magazines in brown wrappers were brought home straight from the post office in a mail-bag by a servant. They were opened and heaped up on my father's desk –

every magazine from *Little Folks* to *Nineteenth Century and After* and *Cornhill*, published in London, was there. My father did not mind our taking away whatever we wanted to read – provided we put them back on his desk without spoiling them, as they had to be placed on the school's reading-room table on Monday morning. So our week-end reading was full and varied. We could dream over the advertisement pages in the *Boys' Own Paper* or the *Strand Magazine*. Through the *Strand* we made the acquaintance of all English writers: Conan Doyle, Wodehouse, W. W. Jacobs, Arnold Bennett, and every English fiction-writer worth the name. The *Bookman* gave us glimpses of the doings of the literary figures of those days, the scene dominated by Shaw, Wells, and Hardy. I knew precisely what they said or thought of each other, how much they earned in royalties, and what they were working on at any given moment. *Obiter dicta*, personal tit-bits about the writers and their world, the Chesterton-Belloc alliance against Shaw or someone else, the scintillating literary world of London was absorbing to watch. From our room, leaning on our pillows in obscure Bojjanna Lines of Mysore, we watched the literary personalities strutting about in London. Through *Harper's*, the *Atlantic*, and *American Mercury*, we attained glimpses of the New World and its writers.

The London *Mercury*, with its orange cover and uncut pages, was especially welcome. I viewed J. C. Squire as if he were my neighbour. *John o' London* and *T. P.'s Weekly* afforded us plenty of literary gossip about publishers and writers. The *Spectator*, the *Times Literary Supplement*, and the *Manchester Guardian* in a thin yellow cover. Twenty-four hours were inadequate for all that one got in hand to read. Slowly, I became familiar with critics who mattered and their judgement. Gradually I began not only to read all the novels in the library but also to acquire through the book reviews a critical sense, so that a certain degree of tempering occurred in my early enthusiasms for some writers – such as Marie Corelli, for instance.

*

I had started writing, mostly under the influence of events occurring around me and in the style of any writer who was uppermost in my mind at the time. My father had lost a dear friend, which affected him deeply. Moved by his sorrow, I wrote ten pages of an outpouring entitled 'Friendship,' very nearly echoing the lamentations of 'Adonais' but in a flamboyant poetic prose. I read this aloud to my younger brother Seenu, who could always be counted upon to utter encouraging words, but I hid it from my elder brother, whose critical sense I feared; and I read my piece also to a few close select friends, who were prepared to walk with me to Kukanahalli Tank, since I always carried my composition in my pocket. Whenever I could afford it, I gave them a cup of coffee at a restaurant on Hundred Feet Road. The cup of coffee blunted the listeners' critical faculties and made them declare my work a masterpiece. When I read it aloud, seated in the shade of the lone tree on Kukanahalli meadow, and heard my words falling on my ears I felt a new thrill each time. At the end of the last line a pregnant silence, while I awaited the good word from my select public.

'Would you like that I should read it again?' I asked, and one or the other said, 'Oh, no. I have absorbed every word.'

'And what do you think of it?'

'I felt the tears coming, but I suppressed them.' Excellent. Precisely what I wished every literary effort to produce. And then: 'Have you read anything similar to this anywhere?'

'This is a rare, unique effort; sometimes reminds me of Shelley's "Adonais" or some of Shakespeare's sonnets.' Precisely,

62

precisely. No comparison would be more welcome and appropriate.

My next effort was 'Divine Music.' I composed it in a state of total abstraction, sitting on a bench at Kukanahalli Tank. I went there one afternoon when the sun was blazing, with a pad and pencil, and filled sheet after sheet even after the sun had set and I could hardly see what my hand was writing: I sit at the edge of the water, listening to the plash of wavelets softly striking the bank. (I later discovered that this was only an unconscious echo of a verse in a Marie Corelli novel which began 'The soft low plash of waves . . . Mariner's voice singing out at sea.') Wavelet after wavelet striking the mud bank, their crests reflecting the full moon – the sight and their soft repeated whispers and the tune of the night breeze induce a sort of self-forgetfulness, in which state I feel an inexplicable aching of the spirit, which churns up a single tear, which rolls down, but before touching the ground is caught between the blades of grass and shines like a diamond or a star. The moment the tear is detached, the sinner's (What sin? I could not really say) repentance is admitted and his soul gains a release; it emerges and fills the space between the stars and beyond, and he hears clearly the music of the spheres. What did it all mean? I don't know. But I was terribly moved and impressed and had no doubt that this was going to add to the world's literary treasure. Naturally my younger brother and the coffee-drinking appreciators endorsed my view. My circle of readers was now enlarging, consequently also the outlay on coffee at the Hundred Feet Road restaurant; I had to seek my mother's help for more pocket money, and she provided it ungrudgingly – an increase from three to five rupees – and that was adequate to forestall any possible hostile reactions and buy favourable opinion. I wrote a third piece without any loss of time. Again it was all about the stars in the sky and floating away on the other side of the stars. I do not remember what I called this piece. This was less successful than the other two when tried on my readers, being a trifle more obscure and mystifying. These efforts were totally unclassifiable – neither poetry, nor prose, nor fiction. Prose in physical form, sound and echo of poetry, and flights of utmost fiction. Odd combination of moods and methods.

I got the pieces copied on demy-sized bond paper, one side only, typed with a generous margin and double-spaced (about all this I learnt from a book named *How to Sell Your Manuscripts*). The typist, who was really a violinist, owned the Venus Typewriting Institute. He was obliging and efficient and charged me (deferred-payment system) two annas a page. When I had typing work, I visited him at his home beside the Jagan Mohan Palace and waited at his door while he ate his morning chupatty, spreading the ghee on it with his finger. Pacing up and down between me and the kitchen, he ate his chapatty unhurryingly. My aim in cornering him at home was to make sure that he did not go away somewhere else to play the violin but proceeded straight to his typewriter. He donned his coat, over his dhoti, wore a fur cap, hooked an umbrella on his arm, and came out. I complimented him on his violin (which he often played solo at our high-school functions), and then spoke about my manuscripts and how I hoped to get them published in London. I flung before him a few names, such as J. C. Squire of the London *Mercury,* Ellis Roberts of *Life and Letters*, R. Scott James of something else. I spoke of them as if they were my chums. We walked through an alley beside the Parakala Temple and reached his little office on Landsdowne Bazaar. He had two typewriters and six students. I had to wait for a machine to be free before he could put paper on the roller. He took about a week to complete my work. Looking at the typed sheets, I felt assured that Scott James or J. C. Squire would have no hesitation in accepting them. I sent them out one by one, after seeking a special grant from my mother for postage and stationery.

The postman became a source of hope at a distance and of despair when he arrived. My interest in him continues even today. In every country I visit, I habitually watch the postman. It's probably a conditioned reflex, like Pavlov's salivating dog. The postman establishes a kind of unity among mankind, even if his uniform differs from country to country. Even in New York, where everything is mechanized and the zip code automatically sorts the mail, the delivery is by hand. In a civilization of complicated mechanism, the postman alone retains the human touch. I stood at our gate at 1087, Bojjanna Lines, on 'foreign mail' days at about three p.m., watching the arrival of the postman around the corner of the co-operative stores at the end of our street. I ran half-way down the street to grab the letters from his hand. I remember his name was Antony – a thin, kindly soul in khaki and turban from whose shoulder enormous bags hung down with parcels sticking out. He waved to me from afar and sometimes cried, 'No letters for you . . .' and asked sometimes, 'Are you waiting for a job or a letter from a girl?' I paused to make sure that he was making no mistake. When he checked and confirmed no letter, I turned back, weighed down with speculation. Could it be that J. C. Squire had flung the manuscripts out of the window, or was there some chicanery somewhere, at the delivery end or the forwarding end, some literary theft? Finally I came to the conclusion that the editor was perhaps reading and rereading 'Divine Music' and was so carried away that he was drafting suggestions for developing it into a full-bodied composition of epic proportions. When the reply actually came, I trembled as I took the packet from Antony's hand. The sun beat down and blinded me in the street, but I had no patience to wait till I reached my room. Moreover, I didn't want my brother and room-mate to see my results. I had already read 'Divine Music' to my brother once and all that he did was to question, 'What does it all mean?' I grinned awkwardly and said, 'Believe me, its meaning must be felt . . .' He merely raised his hand and covered his lips, which were cynically curved. I kept away from him my attempts to reach the London editors. When Antony gave me back my packet, I stood in the shade at the back wall of the co-operative stores and ripped open the envelope, still hoping for a warm letter or a cheque to fall out; but a neatly printed rejection slip was pinned to the manuscript, which otherwise showed no sign of having ever been looked at. It enraged me – the cold, callous rejection slip, impersonal and mocking. Must be a mistake somewhere . . . Perhaps the editor was away and some mean factotum at the office . . . Or why not send it back or why not tell the editor what a dunderhead he must be not to be responsive to 'Divine Music'? How he could run a magazine at all, if he did not mean to read the fine things submitted to him on his own invitation? Typed double space, one side, all conditions honoured. I flung away the rejection slip and the cover into a rubbish dump and putting the manuscript into an inner pocket went back to my room depressed, not mentioning this disgrace – I took it as a personal affront – to anyone. Depression lasted a couple of days, and with renewed hope, only changing the pin, I sent it off again – this time perhaps to Ellis Roberts of *Life and Letters* – remembering how the *Vicar of Wakefield* or some other masterpiece was rejected by ten publishers. Even the masters faced a cold, soul-killing reception at the start of their lives. Reinforced with such thoughts, I was back at the post-office counter at Chamarajapuram, weighing the packet; this time I enclosed with the three manuscripts a personal letter imploring the editor to give himself a chance to read the compositions. I had no doubt that once he surrendered himself to my writing he would become my most passionate champion.

*

In 1926 I passed the university entrance examination and took my seat in the lecture hall of Maharaja's College for my B.A. The college is built in the early French style with octagonal turrets and arched windows on one side and Athenian columns on the other, giving on intoxicating views of the landscape up to the horizon. There was no escape whichever way one turned. A windowed classroom looking out over a landscape is deadly for scholarly concentration. If a student is to listen attentively to lectures he should be cooped up in a windowless classroom in the heart of a city. At Madras the school windows let on a view of nothing more stirring than the wall of the next building, sometimes blank or, worse, plastered with posters. But here in Mysore I found the classroom windows revealing trees and birds, or meadows with cows placidly chewing grass and perhaps the cowherd sitting in the shade. In such a setting, I found the teacher's voice a meaning-less drone, which one had to tolerate perforce. From the eastern corridors of the college, one saw Chamundi Hill in all its fullness framed in arches along the parapet; Maharaja's College was on one ridge of the city, with the hill and the Lalitha Mahal Palace on the other; in the valley in between lay the city with the golden dome of the palace standing out. During the political-science hour, one could watch the shadow of clouds skimming the mountainside, alternating with patches of sunlight, or the mirage shimmering across the landscape, and nothing seemed more irrelevant than the Location of Sovereignty in a Modern State or Checks and Balances in Democracy.

For English literature and history, we had to move to the Greek end of the building, on its western side. Now the view was from a gallery seat through a doorway, between tall, fluted columns; one could see the playground and pavilion bounded by a railway line, with a little train whistling and ambling up and down periodically; there was also a glimpse of the Oriental Library, with friezes depicting the life of God Krishna along its walls and inscribed pillars on its lawns, where once again one noticed cows grazing with concentration and contentment. (There are more cows in Mysore than in any other city, though not milk.) During my college years, I became so familiar with the scenic details and their transformations around that I could have drawn up, if need be, a timetable of the natural events. During June and July, for instance, fitful drizzling alternated with sunlight bursting through the clouds, and a rainbow sometimes arched over the hill. If a painter had attempted to put all these things on his canvas, he would have been berated for overstatement, but Nature, having no such qualms about criticism, was exuberant and profuse and distracted my attention from my lessons.

I missed a great deal that went on in the classroom, with a couple of exceptions. Shakespeare, taught by Professor Rollo, was enjoyable and edifying. Tall and graceful, Rollo looked like an actor and he read the lines in different tones effectively. He did exquisite monologues. When he trailed and swept his (academic) gown and paced up and down on the platform, you heard the king's voice; when he wrapped his gown close, you heard the fool's remarks, and got at the meaning of Shakespeare's verse. Professor Rollo was an ideal teacher. Even now, from somewhere in Cheshire, he occasionally writes to his old students. The only other professor who sounded interesting was Professor Venkateswara, who taught us Indian history. His home was across the playfield, and only after he heard the bell for his hour did he leave his study. We crowded beside the Greek column and watched the football field while he emerged on the horizon, clad in dhoti, academic gown, and turban. He had a portly figure and arrived unhurryingly, always late by a quarter of an hour, and entered the lecture hall muttering an apology for being late. When settled, he would produce from somewhere a small strip of paper with a few lines of ancient inscription copied on it. 'I came across these lines . . .' – they could be Asoka's edicts carved on rocks and pillars dated 250 B.C. or a Mughal chronicler's note – but it was always engrossing, bordering on fiction, and would be the starting point of his lecture. He never proceeded chronologically but pursued several channels of historical facts and parallel concepts simultaneously. He would not notice the time passing or the bell going off at the end of his hour, but continue and encroach on the next hour, while Professor Toby hovered outside and made several infructuous attempts to step in and teach Greek drama or eighteenth-century poetry. Professor Toby was shy and timid, looked exactly like Laurel of Laurel and Hardy, and he constantly stroked his chin as if in perplexity. We would not, however, feel sorry that his lectures were delayed, as his teaching made one's mind wander, even if one's body could not actually slip out and relax on the pedestal of Asoka Pillar at the Oriental Library. His accents were peculiar and we never understood a word of his lecture in the class. For his part he never lifted his head or looked at anyone, nor did he take the roll-call, being unable to pronounce a single Indian name. For many years, it was rumoured that he had thought that he was teaching at a women's college, mistaking the men's dhotis for skirts and their tufts for braids. He was a good man, though, and many a venturesome young man visited his house and pleading poverty took loans from him. Since he never looked up or knew a name, he never identified his borrowers and lost money regularly. He spent over a quarter-century in this same isolation, retired, and was not heard of again. His parting message on the last day of his lecture was, 'I hope your interest in literature will not vanish with the examinations,' or some similar-sounding words. With this farewell, he hopped off the platform and was gone. We lost sight of him after his retirement. A few years ago, however, I was in Leeds and took a trip to visit the home of the Brontë sisters. There I noticed him in a hat shop, trying on a bowler hat. As usual his eyes were fixed like a yogi's on the ground, and he was stroking his chin in perplexity. I was on the point of hailing him across the counter, but he left abruptly and I saw him no more.

My inseparable friend at the college was Ramachandra Rao. Slight of build and only five feet tall, wearing thick lenses, he was endowed with an ebullient nature. He sat beside me on the class bench, joined me again for a four-mile walk towards the hill, shared my cigarette expenses, jokes, and observations, and was full of humour and laughter. As the final exams approached we 'joint-studied.' After dinner I walked to his home in Santhepet, a couple of miles away, a vast household teeming with many cousins and aunts where he managed to keep a room for himself. We sat down methodically at nine o'clock, determined to get through Hazen's *European History* or Gilchrist's political theories before the night ended – a fight to a finish with the subject, the heart of the matter to be wrenched out of the book, to recoup all that we had missed in the classroom. One of us read, the other listened by turns – thus we hoped to relieve the tedium of study. But in practice, hardly had one of us read ten pages when the other would interrupt with an observation, 'Why waste time on this portion? We won't have any question on Italian unity this year. It was given two years in succession – skip it. Bismarck is more likely.' Arguments for and against this view. We would decide to take a quick glance through Italian unity, skipping details, not the heart of the matter but just the outline of the heart. Resuming the study after this interlude, we would start off again and come to a halt when something else came to mind, perhaps the amours of Maria Theresa, or some reminiscences of the classroom, or the farewells on the last day after the 'social gathering,' and the group photo. After all this recollection in tranquillity, one of us would notice the Hazen lying open and suddenly declare, 'I say, only fifteen days left! Even if we devote twenty hours a day, we will never finish the portions.' We would be seized with panic and resolve: 'Let us sit up till six a.m. if necessary and finish European history, so that we may go on to other subjects.'

'Quite right. What if we don't sleep? Let us have all the sleep after April.'

'What about Indian history? Luckily no Greek history this year. Otherwise you would have six hundred pages of Bury!'

'Why go into that now?'

'We must get someone to summarize all the subjects in ten pages each. We must request Seenu to do it; after all, he has no public exam this year.'

Seenu, one year our junior in class, always obliging, would willingly undertake such literary tasks (as he still does, as a secretary for whichever maharaja or governor happens to employ him at the moment). This was a sudden, agreeable solution to our problems, bringing such a relief to our minds that we would shut the book and go out in search of a tea shop. A leisurely walk through the streets, marvelling at the tranquil air that the city wore at night, and after one or two cigarettes, we would return to our desk past midnight. Hazen again, but presently Nature would assert itself and make us nod; we would realize that 'joint study' was a waste of time and that we should study separately if at all and meet occasionally to discuss and clear doubts, or better still watch for any secret leakage of the question papers through the devious and dark agencies operating in Bangalore, a city full of adventurous possibilities. And so good-night, one precious day out of the fifteen before the examination gone irrevocably.

*

Nineteen-thirty, when I attained a belated graduation, became a year of problems. What should one do with oneself now? Different suggestions came in from different quarters. One could become a lawyer, or a minor civil servant, or what not. At first I toyed with the idea of studying for an M.A. degree in literature and becoming a college lecturer. While I was going up the stairs of the Maharaja's College with my application for a seat in the M.A. class, a friend met me half-way and turned me back, arguing that this would be a sure way to lose interest in literature. I accepted his advice and went downstairs, once for all turning my back on college studies.

SEVEN

IT WAS INCONCEIVABLE that one should stay at home without some office to attend after graduation. The right thing would be to apply for jobs and meet influential persons, to knock on all doors of employment. My father had an old friend at Madras who ended up as the Chief Auditor of Railways but who in his college days had been hard up and was helped with clothes and money by my father. My father had immense hopes that his old friend would now help me. We were in Madras during the summer of that year. My father was insistent that I should meet his friend and seek his help for an appointment in the railways. One morning, neatly groomed and dressed, I started out to meet this man, putting on as mild and affable a look as possible, already imagining myself lording it over station masters and travelling in a saloon-car all over India freely. The gentleman was bare-bodied and glistened with an oil-coating, as he prepared himself for a massage; he blinked several times to make me out, as oil had dripped over his eyes and blurred his vision. He met me half-way across the front verandah of his house, where no man in his senses would let himself be seen by a visitor in that messy state, and unceremoniously shouted, not 'Who?' but 'What?' All my best efforts at grooming were wasted, for I must have looked to him like a photograph taken with a shivering hand. I explained my mission, citing my father's friendship with him. 'Oh!' he cried looking outraged through his half-closed eyes. 'What a notion! Impossible. Your father was always a dreamer. This is not a job for you. What was your optional subject for B.A.?'

'History, economics, and politics.' He looked at me with distaste. 'No use,' he declared. 'What class? What rank?' I trembled inwardly at the question and dodged a direct answer. 'They have not announced the classes yet.' He waved me off and resumed his impatient pacing like a greasy bear in its cage.

My father next sent me on a similar errand to another friend who had retired from bank service. I did not take to this suggestion with any zest. I had had no misgivings about travelling in a saloon-car as a railway officer, but I had grave ones when I thought of myself as a bank official. I never felt at ease with figures. But I still went to this friend, as my father desired, another morning, well groomed and properly dressed. This man, though not oily, was also bare-bodied (everyone seemed to be shirtless in Madras). He was fanning himself with a palmyra leaf, sitting on a swing, while I kept standing. It was difficult to carry on a conversation with him as he approached and receded on his swing. I had to adjust my voice in two pitches to explain my mission and also step back each time the swing came for me. Like the previous gentleman, this man also figured in a group photo of select friends framed and hung in my father's study at Mysore. He also seemed to loathe history and economics and said, 'You must pass some book-keeping and accountancy if you wish to try for a bank job. How does your father spend his time nowadays? He used to be such a fop!' He added, 'He wrote to me that he has retired from service now. Now it is up to you young fellows to take over the family responsibilities . . .'

Well said, I thought. But that precisely is our problem now, sir. Why don't you put your shirt on and do something about it, instead of swinging back and forth in that silly manner advising people?

*

My father had retired from service a year or two before, and it had meant all sort of readjustments at home. His pension was meagre, and we had to move on to a cheaper house in Laxmipuram, leaving Bojjanna Lines, where I had spent the dreamiest of my years. The Laxmipuram house was smaller, less roomy, two small hexagonal rooms in the front part, separated by a short veranda; one was occupied by my father, and the parallel room by me and my elder brother, as usual, where we had the advantage of watching a very pretty neighbour as she bent over her studies in her room upstairs, clearly visible from our window; that she was not distracted by our attention was proved when eventually she won first class in several subjects in the B.A. and received medals at the convocation in the same year as I took my degree lost in a back row.

Our room had a broad wooden staircase which led nowhere. I used its top landing for storing a monstrous typewriter that I had acquired at Madras and had brought with me in a capacious linen basket, since it was presented to me without a cover. It looked like a computer. It had separate keys for capital and lower cases; and its carriage moved with a big boom. All afternoon I sat on the landing and typed a play called *Prince Yazid*, the story of an independent-minded Mughal prince who was tortured and tormented by his father. After several decades, this was recently returned to me from the office of my literary agent, David Higham, where it had been discovered among their destroyable papers, and one may judge of its career from this simple fact. The entire staircase rocked and boomed when I was at work, and my father sometimes protested against the noise, whereupon I would have to haul the machine over to the roof of the house and type there. My brother Seenu, as ever, helped me with typing the play and often quoted lines from it admiringly. If I am not mistaken, he was the only reader of *Prince Yazid*. All this amount of desperate composition was to allow me to earn money and help the family. My father still had three of my younger brothers at school, and Seenu himself in M.A.; Seenu still remembers his first day in M.A. when his professor, teaching Indian culture, began, 'Culture is of different kinds: agriculture, physical culture, sericulture, and so forth. But we must distinguish between cultures and find out their common characteristics and differences. All culture is one.' In spite of this teacher, Seenu persisted in his M.A. studies, as they would mean a better market value for him than a mere B.A. My elder brother worked in a radio-repair shop and then as the manager of a bus service, and was away the whole day until midnight; he added fifty rupees a month to the family budget. My father occasionally enquired of me, 'What are you attempting on that road-roller?' (my typewriter). He gently suggested that I should not be wasting my time thus.

Having nothing to do in Mysore, I moved off to Bangalore and stayed with my grandmother, who was there to recoup her health; and so back again under the care of my grandmother after many years' interval. I wandered about the streets of Bangalore, dreaming and thinking and planning. On a certain day in September, selected by my grandmother for its auspiciousness, I bought an exercise book and wrote the first line of a novel; as I sat in a room nibbling my pen and wondering what to write, Malgudi with its little railway station swam into view, all ready-made, with a character called Swaminathan running down the platform peering into the faces of passengers, and grimacing at a bearded face; this seemed to take me on the right track of writing, as day by day pages grew out of it linked to each other. (In the final draft the only change was that the Malgudi Station came at the end of the story.) This was a satisfactory beginning for me, and I regularly wrote a few pages each day.

At about this time one of my father's efforts to place me bore fruit. I received a government order appointing me as a teacher at a government school in our old Chennapatna, where I used to spend my vacations as a schoolboy. So I was going back one fine morning by train from Mysore to the land of my grasshopper collections. I was seen off at Mysore with great enthusiasm by everyone in the family; everybody was happy that I was to work in Chennapatna, familiar ground, only half-way between Mysore and Bangalore; it would be like being in both places at once. Many were the benefits and blessings of being posted to Chennapatna rather than anywhere else, and of course I caught a part of their enthusiasm and had pictured Chennapatna as a haven of pleasant prospects. But the memories and impressions created in childhood could be very misleading. My train arrived at Chennapatna at about ten-thirty in the morning, and I had to climb into a jutka with a roll of bedding and my trunk, and drive straight to the high school in order to report for duty before eleven. The government order had said, 'You must report yourself in the forenoon on the first of December.' This was the first of December, and forenoon. I paid off the jutka and left my baggage on the school veranda and went into the headmaster's room, announced myself, and signed a register of service. The headmaster gave me a few words of welcome and advice, and sent me off to a sixth-form class to teach Tennyson's 'Morte d'Arthur.' I had no notion how I should teach. An old servant of the school, whom we used to call Venkata, followed me uttering advice in a menacing undertone. He had survived since the days of my father's headmastership. He said in a warning manner, 'Take care that you don't let down your great father's reputation.' He used to escort us when we were children during our evening walks, and now did not seem to recognize that

I was a grown-up and a teacher appointed by the government. He warned me, 'If you don't maintain the reputation of my old master, I will not let you off lightly, remember!' While I took my seat in the teacher's chair, he stood at the door surveying me with great satisfaction, and nodded his head approvingly when I tapped the table with my hands and cried, 'Silence!' Somehow it had an effect. An eerie silence ensued as the boys studied their new master with interest. 'Page seventy . . . I hope all of you have your copies ready. Never come to the class without your books,' I said, discovering a new principle for myself. 'I am very strict about it.'

'Yes sir,' said a few voices in a chorus. I didn't like it. Perhaps they were being ironical. There was a tall Muslim boy in a last row. I looked at him and said, 'You read out on page seventy.' He got up. Too old for his class. He was slow in taking out his book and turning the pages. The boys looked around with smiling faces. I didn't know why. The tall boy was also smiling without reading out. I felt I had committed a mistake, but how could a teacher go back on his command? 'What is your name?' I asked.

'Anweruddin.'

'Anweruddin,' I said, 'I hope you have your poetry book.'

'No sir,' he said.

'Then what is that book in your hand?'

He held it up for me to see. I could not make out at this distance what he was displaying.

'Bring it here,' I said. He stepped forward and walked up. The class was enjoying the scene. I could hear giggling and whispers. I took it and said, 'Why don't you try and fetch the right book? I don't like people coming in without their books.' I had enunciated a principle and had to stick to it. Moreover, old Venkata's words about living up to my father's reputation still rankled in my mind. I was going to prove who was the real master here. He hesitated, and I said rather firmly, 'Now you may go and fetch the poetry book if you have left it somewhere.'

'Yes sir,' he said and turned on his heels and went back to his seat. Giggles and whispers and a mild excitement running through the class. I felt victorious. On the very first occasion one should establish one's superiority. If that was delayed, one would forever be taken for a milksop. In spite of the giggling, I felt relieved at the prompt manner in which Anweruddin had obeyed me. Now he came back from his seat holding up the right book. I didn't ask for any explanation of his conduct; it was not necessary. I met his challenge by briskly taking the book, turning to page seventy, and saying, 'Now read aloud to the class, face the class.' Still with a leer, he took the book, but instead of reading said, 'Please let me go out,' and held up his forefinger, which indicates from time immemorial that one wants to be let out for 'Number One.' I had done the same thing at Lutheran Mission whenever I wished to leave the classroom; and the worst teacher in the world cannot reject that request. I let him go. He walked off majestically, but before the class could continue in this mood of entertainment, I read out, ' "So all day long the noise of battle roll'd/ . . . until King Arthur's table . . ." ' et cetera et cetera. A few boys listened to my reading, a few talked among themselves. I raised the pitch of my voice and, 'This poem by Tennyson . . .' Two more boys stood in their seats holding up their forefingers. 'Yes,' I said, and announced, 'Whoever wishes to go out, may go, but don't disturb the other classes.' Half the class walked out and never came back, and I read on about twenty lines, wondering in what manner I should explain their meaning to whoever cared to stay. They didn't seem to care for Tennyson or anyone, but were chatting among themselves. Luckily for me the bell rang, and thus concluded my first experience of teaching. It was also perhaps the last.

Soon I got into trouble with the headmaster. He sent me next to a fifth form to handle a physics class. When I pleaded that I was a history man, he brushed aside my objection and said that since the physics teacher was absent, I should take on his duties and keep the class engaged. It sounded silly to me, but I obeyed him. The fifth-form juniors were a more disorderly crowd than the sixth-form boys whom I had taught first. The boys kept pouncing on each other, grabbing, flinging their caps in the air, shouting challenges, and denouncing one another; it looked less like a classroom, more like a festival crowd on rampage. I wondered if the physics teacher purposely kept away rather than deal with these young devils. I resented the headmaster's devilry in sending me into this confusion on my very first day.

I hammered the table with my fist several times and shouted, 'Silence, silence!' That produced silence for a brief second while the boys paused to stare at the teacher with wonder and contempt. Then they resumed the hubbub, which rose like an ocean's roar, fifty boys jabbering away at different pitches. I watched them for a little while and said, 'You must all write a composition now, ten lines on how you spent your last holiday, now out with your notebooks and pencils, come on.' A handful displayed some response, and took out their notebooks and turned the pages and bit their pencil points, but many others, watching these conformists with interest, made no move to start writing. I repeated the theme of the composition and then added, 'Whoever has finished the writing may show it to me and go.' This was a good incentive as presently they all came over to my table and piled their notebooks on it. I felt smothered, to read fifty compositions! I quickly added, 'Take away your notebooks and leave. Show them to me later.' 'When?' someone asked, and before I could muster an answer they left their notebooks on the table and fled like a flock of released birds. I painstakingly collected the notebooks and left them in the custody of the school clerk at the administrative office. I spent the rest of the day in the room of a colleague who was trying to guide me in this wilderness. We went for a walk in the evening along the bazaar, and dined at a restaurant – which was the dirtiest in my experience, the food being served on a dried banana leaf spread out on the floor of a dusty back veranda. I bore it patiently, my friend saying, 'In a week you can ask for a room at the school hostel. At the moment there is no vacancy.' Next morning I was back trying to teach English to the sixth form again when a servant brought me a register to sign. I thought at first that it might be some routine office memo, but when I looked carefully, it said, 'You are hereby warned that your letting off of the Fifth A was unauthorized and is likely to affect the discipline of the school. If there is a repetition of such an act, matter will be reported to higher authorities. This is the first warning.' It was signed by the headmaster. The servant insisted on my signing it. I pushed it away saying, 'No, I won't.' When the hour ended, I stormed into the headmaster's room. He said, 'You have returned the register without signing. It is your service register,' and he pushed it towards me. I signed it with an angry flourish.

'Is there anything else?' I asked. 'Give me anything, I will sign it. I am only a day old in service and you want me to start my career with a black mark, is it?'

'Oh, no, don't take it to heart, young man. It is just a formality, a formal record. It means nothing.'

'I don't care either way. I want fifteen days' leave.'

'You are not entitled to any leave yet.'

'Leave without pay.'

'You can't take any sort of leave.'

This irritated me and I said haughtily, 'I am going away and you may do what you like.'

The headmaster softened. 'Don't be rash, young man. You must learn by experience; you will understand in due course that these things do not matter. You must do your duty with conscience and diligence. Of course we are here to help you if you have any difficulties. We are interested in seeing you prosper. Don't do anything rash. These days are difficult for Brahmins to get jobs in the government.'

'I know Mr. Wadia and he was my professor and my father's friend; I can ask him for a transfer.' The mention of this name shook the headmaster. He became pale. Wadia was the Director of Public Instruction and at the apex of the entire educational edifice.

'Don't do anything rash. If you would like to go away on Friday afternoon, I will make some special concession and see what I can do. Spend two days at home, but be back on Monday noon. I will see that you have no class until noon.' He was scared out of his wits, he felt I might complain and get him into trouble. I did not wait until Friday afternoon. An hour later, I stood at the bus stand with my trunk and roll of bedding, waiting for a bus to take me to Mysore. I felt a little nervous lest my colleagues should discover me under the tree on the roadside by which the bus was to pass. Some people passed unnoticing; a few students of the high school, passing, looked at me curiously. Suddenly hefty Anweruddin turned up with a couple of his followers and stood before me, his eyes full of surprise. I could not pretend not to notice him. He saluted me courteously and grinned. I asked, 'What are you doing here instead of being in your class?'

'We had no class, sir, the teacher was absent. *You* had to teach us at this hour.' He appeared grateful that I had helped him to wander about freely. 'Why, sir, where are you going?'

'To Mysore. I am not coming back. Go and tell the headmaster that you saw me go away.' Anweruddin looked unhappy at the parting and mumbled something. He lifted my baggage and placed it on the bus when it arrived and stood aside morosely until the bus started. 'Good-bye, sir,' he said, rather subdued, and made a deep salaam.

*

Back at home in Mysore, I became an object of much speculation. They seemed to suspect my sanity. I spent most of my time lounging on a canvas chair in my room for fear of being asked to explain myself. I was tired of the subject and avoided people. My mother, who could always be counted upon to be sympathetic, said, 'Your father is very worried about you. Chennapatna is an inexpensive place; I'm sure if you stuck on, you would get a higher grade and save enough to make you comfortable and spare for others too. Your father will speak to Wadia and see if you can be transferred to a Mysore school soon. It will be helpful to everyone. But you must be patient for some time.' She was persuasive, and it disturbed my complacency a little. I went back to my brooding chamber to think it over. I avoided encountering my father by staying in my room. He was not the kind to intrude into our domains. But one afternoon he suddenly called, 'Kunjappa [my name in domestic circles]! Come here.' He was in the hall. He looked up at me with some amusement and said, 'What do you propose to do?' He jingled his key-bunch. 'Give Chennapatna another trial. Not a bad place. I have spoken to people and they will treat you with special consideration. I have also spoken to Mukund Rao, who has his brother at Chennapatna in a bank, and he will put you up at his home until you get used to the place, until you can make some other arrangement. Good people. You will feel at home.' His attitude seemed to have changed. He had never sounded more friendly in his life.

So I decided to give Chennapatna another trial. Mr. Mukund Rao, a minor official in the Revenue Department, but practically my father's devoted slave for thirty years since his student days, saw me off at the railway station with many words of advice. I was received at the other end by his replica, his brother, in a close coat and lace-edged turban, who took charge of me without a word, placed my baggage on a coolie's head, conducted me to his house, just fifteen minutes from the railway station. (Oh, that was a pleasant discovery, not too far to go if I wished to take a train back to Mysore!) This man and his young wife occupied a small house – mud-walled, lime-washed, with a low tiled roof, smoky and ancient – in a side-street of Chennapatna Town. You could see the school building, too, from his little window. Their house had a little front room, and a back room which served as kitchen. Those two were the meekest pair I have ever met in my life. The wife was orthodox and would not come before a stranger except to serve food, and would not look at you or speak. That was understandable, being a part of a lady's good behaviour, but what I could not understand was why the gentleman was equally meek and speechless. He seemed to have surrendered his only room to me and kept himself mostly on the front steps leading to the street. I was, perhaps, the first guest in their lives, and they looked panicky, concerned, and overwhelmed. I seemed to have shaken the equanimity of their lives and caused them a profound disturbance. The man left after our first meal – no word being spoken during, before, or after it. Soon after eating, he picked up a coat and turban, went into the kitchen, and came out dressed for his bank. I sat on the floor leaning against the inevitable roll of bedding that I had carried with me. He whispered timidly an adieu and left. His wife concealed herself in the kitchen. I was oppressed with the thought that I had, perhaps, imposed myself on this light, birdlike couple. I had still an hour for the school. I dressed and left, announcing my departure by pulling the street door behind me with a bang; the lady stole up softly from the kitchen and bolted it. I imagined that she might now sing and dance to celebrate the exit (though temporary) of her guest.

At school, a repetition of my previous performance. Old Venkata demanded to know where I had gone, and I told him I had had fever. The additional worry this time was that I was asked to conduct drill for some class at the end of the day. I protested. The headmaster said, 'Every member of the staff is expected to handle drill classes once a week by turn.'

'I don't know any drill – never attended any class even as a schoolboy.'

'Keep them engaged for an hour. Don't let them off. We are trying to teach them also *Surya Namaskar*.'

'I know nothing about it.'

'We will help you to learn it by and by. Today keep them engaged. Take the roll-call and make note of the absentees.'

And so I found myself in the drill field surveying an array of fifty boys standing in two rows under the evening sun. The sun hit us from the west. Many others, including teachers, stood around to watch my performance. I inspected the boys closely, like a commander reviewing an army, cried 'Right, left, right, left,' marched them, made them perform high jumps, long jumps, swing their arms, kick their legs in the air. I engaged them as long as I could; still no bell rang to indicate the end of the hour. I cried, 'Stand at ease!' and then, 'Dismissed!' and the whole crowd vanished in a second.

I slept in my host's house in the hall, the meek man curling up in a corner, and his wife sleeping beside the oven on the kitchen floor, perhaps. I felt guilty to be separating the pair thus. In the morning it was especially embarrassing to get started with one's washing and toilet since they had a minimal arrangement for such activities. The latrine was at the back yard, four dwarfish mud walls screening you but without a door, open to the sky; you were visible outside over the short wall until you squatted down. I had a fear of being seen by the lady in this situation. For my bath, I had to go behind a tin screen. My host and hostess kept themselves rigorously in the background while I was getting through my ablutions, but still I felt extremely nervous and exposed to public view.

I got ready for the school. The man left for his bank. I suddenly felt it would be impossible to spend another day at school or in this house. I knew the bus would be coming in half an hour under the tree. Got a coolie to carry my box and roll of bedding, banged the street door until the lady came up behind it, mentioned to her I was leaving for Mysore, and caught the bus for Mysore again.

EIGHT

THAT SETTLED IT. After the final and irrevocable stand I took, I felt lighter and happier. I did not encourage anyone to comment on my deed or involve myself in any discussion. I sensed that I was respected for it. At least there was an appreciation of the fact that I knew my mind. I went through my day in a business-like manner, with a serious face. Soon after my morning coffee and bath I took my umbrella and started out for a walk. I needed the umbrella to protect my head from the sun. Sometimes I carried a pen and pad and sat down under the shade of a tree at the foot of Chamundi Hill and wrote. Some days I took out a cycle and rode ten miles along the Karapur Forest Road, sat on a wayside culvert, and wrote or brooded over life and literature, watching some peasant ploughing his field, with a canal flowing glitteringly in the sun. My needs were nil, I did not have plans, there was a delight in being just alive and free from employment. That was a great luxury. I returned home at noon in time for lunch, read something inconsequential for an hour or two. I took care not to read too much or anything that might influence my writing at the moment. I was trying to progress with my first novel. At three o'clock after a cup of coffee I wrote. Day by day *Swami* was developing. The pure delight of watching a novel grow can never be duplicated by any other experience. I cannot recollect how much I wrote each day, perhaps a few hundred words, or a thousand. Swami, my first character, grew up and kept himself alive and active; the novel was episodic, but that was how it naturally shaped itself; a series of episodes, escapades, and adventures of Swami and his companions. Each day as I sat down to write, I had no notion of what would be coming. All that I could be certain of was the central character. I reread the first draft at night to make out how it was shaping and undertook, until far into the night, corrections, revisions, and tightening up of sentences. I began to notice that the sentences acquired a new strength and finality while being rewritten, and the real, final version could emerge only between the original lines and then again in what developed in the jumble of rewritten lines, and above and below them. It was, on the whole, a pleasant experience – which is later lost, to some extent, when one becomes established, with some awareness of one's publishers, methods, transactions, the trappings of publicity and reviews, and above all a public.

I had to have an objective test of what I was doing, and so I gave my manuscript to Seenu, as usual, who offered not only to read but also to type it on my elephantine machine. He became quite engrossed in the characters and said several good things about the book. That was most encouraging. But still I wanted other tests. So I summoned my neighbour, a very warm-hearted friend named Purna, who is no more, to come up and listen to me while I read out the chapters to him each day. He went on crying, 'Brilliant, brilliant!' He knew no lesser expression than 'brilliant,' and that was very sustaining. It shielded me against the sly attacks from my father's friends when they met me in the street. 'Unwisdom! unwisdom!' one of my father's friends would say and add, 'You must not cause all this worry to your father. This is a time when you should help him. Why don't you join a newspaper if you want to be a writer?'

Most of my father's friends did not know the difference between a novel and a newspaper, yet I explained, 'I want to finish my novel, and when it is published, it will solve all problems. Until then one has to wait.' I still had no conception of myself as an economic entity.

'Unwisdom, unwisdom!' the gentleman cried. 'You could write as a hobby, how can you make a living as a writer? The notion is very unpractical.'

This was more or less the tenor of everybody's advice to me, but it was impossible for me to acquire a view of myself as an economic entity. I did not have even a rupee at my command. The only luxury that I indulged in was smoking – two cigarettes a day while walking in the evenings. Gold Flake cost in those days only two pice each, and if I had a couple of annas for my expenses each day, I was quite satisfied, and did not look for more.

From time to time an uncle, my mother's younger brother (known as 'Junior,' the one who brought me up at Madras being the 'Senior'), visited us and stayed at our house for weeks on end. We always felt happy at his arrival. He was an automobile salesman and his pockets burst with cash. He took us to restaurants and for long car drives, bought us whatever we asked for – clothes, shoes, odds and ends. He loved eating, and brought baskets filled with vegetables and foodstuff and fruits home from the market. He was very devoted to my mother, and kept us free from financial worries, at least when he stayed with us. He always carried a tin of cigarettes and we had the use of it. Although it was inconceivable that one could smoke in an uncle's presence, one could have his cigarettes and the uncle would only joke about it.

But he drank a lot every evening and behaved wildly. He would insist on our company in the evenings while out driving his car, but he sat till ten o'clock at the bar, and when returning home, threatened to run over every pedestrian and scare him off the street, argued with every policeman at traffic points, attempted to take his car up the steps of the Maharaja's statue at the palace gate, and came home late. My father discreetly kept himself in his own room at such moments, since he knew that my uncle had much regard for him. My father was very puritanical, and though his adversaries alleged – because of his fair complexion flushed red when cycling down to school, and his gruff voice – that he came to school drunk, he was a teetotaller and tolerated a drunken brother-in-law only out of consideration for my mother.

After dinner this drunken uncle settled down to a nice chat with the family and insisted on having everyone around him. He enjoyed teasing me and Seenu, but left alone my elder brother, who would spurn him at such moments. He would ask Seenu: 'Did you buy betel leaves at the market?' which he would want for chewing after dinner.

'Yes, *Mama*.'

'How many leaves were in the bundle?'

'One hundred, as you wanted . . .'

'Did you count the leaves in the bundle?'

'But the woman who sold it counted . . .'

'You mean to say that you took her word for it? Ha, ha, very well. Count it now . . . Go on.' Seenu would be bullied into counting the leaves, one by one, loudly, watched over by the uncle. If the bundle contained ninety-nine, he would glare at Seenu and say, 'Now go to the market and get the remaining one'; or if Seenu counted one hundred and one, he would be ordered, 'Take the extra one leaf and give it back to the woman. We must not cheat her.'

'All right. When?'

'Now, this minute. It will teach you to be careful when you buy anything in the market.' Market being two miles away and the time being near midnight, this was a reckless suggestion, but my brother said 'Yes' and vanished, quietly shut himself in his room, and studied his lessons.

Uncle's teasing of me, however, took a different turn at these assemblies. He would suddenly say, 'Do I hear aright when people say that you plan to be a writer?' I could not say 'Yes' or 'No.' There was danger in either. I wished that I could leave the scene as my brother did, but Uncle would feel outraged if he were abandoned thus and become theatrical and upset my mother, who needed our presence at this moment. When I confirmed his suspicion that I wished to be a writer, he would demand to see what I was writing. Urged by my mother, who somehow felt that it would help me in some way, I would show him the typed sheets. He held one to the light and read out, ' "It was Monday morning." Oh, oh, Monday! Why not Tuesday or Friday?' He glanced through the others and said, 'What the hell is this? You write that he got up, picked up tooth powder, rinsed his teeth, poured water over his head – just a catalogue! H'm. I could also write a novel if all that is expected of me is to say that I got up, picked up a towel, rubbed the soap, dried myself, shook off the water, combed . . . I could also become a novelist if this was all that was expected, but I have no time to write a detailed catalogue. And what's this Malgudi? Where is it? Why do you write about some vague place not found anywhere, while there are millions of real places you can write about? Don't write about unreal places. You must read Dickens' novels. You chaps think you are all very clever. I have read every line Dickens has written. There you have a model, write like him.'

I bore all this patiently. As a reward for my patience, he offered to introduce me to some persons in the writing line so that I might make some money – even if I wasn't going to be a good writer. During his next visit to Bangalore, he took me along in his car, determined to help me in spite of my notions.

In addition to my novel, I had on hand about twenty short stories written mainly to see if other subjects than love (which appeared to be the sole theme for every novel, short story, poem, or drama in existence) could be written about. I wished to attack the tyranny of Love and see if Life could offer other values than the inevitable Man–Woman relationship to a writer. I found in the short-story pages of *John o' London*'s stories which appealed to me, themes centering around a moment or a mood with a crisis. I found in the life around me plenty of material. The atmosphere and mood were all-important. Life offered enough material to keep me continuously busy. I could write one story a day. I noted in a diary possible themes, and developed them at my leisure, whenever I felt the need for a change from the novel. In addition to this, I also wrote in about two hundred words, each day, a little essay of impressions or vignettes – these were often flimsy, affected, and self-conscious, echoes of something I had been reading, but it was a good exercise and a daily discipline. Thus I had quite a handful to show any publisher who might take an interest in me – a novel in progress, short stories, skits, and essays.

My uncle took me here and there in Bangalore. 'Mysore is no good, a sleepy place. If you want to get on, seek your prospects in a city like Bangalore or Madras,' he would say. He took me out with him every morning in his car. He drove his demonstration car nearly a hundred miles a day, saw dozens of persons, subjected them to his sales-talk, and booked at least one order a day and celebrated his success with four gins before lunch. He kept me in his company throughout, and I acquired valuable experience and familiarity with a variety of human types, their style of talk and outlook. Above all, my uncle himself was an inescapable model for me – his approach to other human beings, his aggressive talk wherever he went, his dash and recklessness (he had had the unique record of taking the Maharaja of Mysore, an absolutely inaccessible recluse, hedged in with security and protocol, for a demonstration in his car); especially his abandon to alcohol in every form all through the day. (I portrayed him as Kailas, in *The Bachelor of Arts*, and he provided all the substance whenever I had to portray a drunken character.) Once, as a result of imbibing a full bottle of George IV whiskey during a motor trip to Nilgiri Mountain, he flung the bottle out into a valley, crying, 'What the hell is an empty doing here?' and later had a conviction that he was turning into a tiger and snarled and stalked behind strangers in the hotel corridor the whole evening until sleep overcame him.

Now, at Bangalore, he mentioned a crony of his whom he described as one interested in 'all sorts of arts – writer and journalist and a man who has published many books and articles. I'm sure he will help you. Unless you get in touch with other writers, how can you hope to get started?' But I gathered later that this literatus's chief source of livelihood was through acting as a broker. For every 'prospect' that he introduced to my uncle, he received fifty rupees and a couple of drinks if he happened to be around at drinking time. He was addressed as 'Prince,' as he claimed to be a member of the Cochin Royal Family. He sat beside my uncle in the car, and I heard their talk from the back seat and learnt much about life in general. At a party my uncle once got into a fight with this Prince. During the scuffle the Prince tugged and tore my uncle's shirt; my uncle immediately left in order to search for an iron rod, swearing to crack his skull. Sensing danger, swiftly the Prince fled by a back stair and ran for his life down the road to his house and shut himself in. With the iron rod clutched in his hand and finding his prey gone, my uncle ran down to his car, started it, drove up and rammed the gate of the Prince's house with the car, demolished a portion of his wall, and challenged: 'Open the door, you bastard Prince . . .' The man kept himself in determinedly, whereupon my uncle turned his car round and came

straight away came to business. 'I hear from your uncle that you want to be a writer. Good. But don't expect to become a millionaire in a day. Remember that the world is not waiting to read your stuff, whatever it may be. People have better things to do. But you must work hard and by sheer persistence, draw their attention to yourself – which means write, write, and write.' After this gratuitous advice, he made his offer. 'At the moment, I have no notion what you write or how. But your uncle is a dear friend and I'll take his word.' He paused to sweep aside the papers on his table and shouted through the window, 'Hey, bring two *colours* immediately.' And immediately on his table were placed by an urchin two bottles of some red aerated water fizzing and hissing like a cobra. 'You must be thirsty, drink that *colour*. It's good.' He set an example by tilting his head back and practically sucking the water out of the bottle, which he thrust between his lips. He put it down, belched loudly, pressed his nostrils with his fingers and said, 'I want to start a magazine solely devoted to matrimonial themes. Marriage is the most serious situation everyone has to face sooner or later, and few give the subject enough thought. Many are the problems that arise before, during, and after a marriage. Two strangers come together and have to live for the rest of their lives. Our journal will be devoted solely to this subject. We want jokes, stories, philosophies, and reflections all on this theme – of women who suffer, of men who are callous, and so on and so forth. You may write anything on these lines. Come back with some material as soon as you can and then we'll talk further.' My head was in the clouds when I returned home that evening.

*

For the next three days, sitting beside my grandmother, I wrote and soon produced several pages of interesting anecdotes and a variety of imaginary stories centering around matrimonial life:

about wife-beaters, husband-baiters, a live-and-let-live couple who faced some calamity, young runaways, elopers and elopees, and every kind of permutation and combination of man and woman. The tone, for some reason, emphasized misery – if not tragedy. It seemed so hard to find a happy couple in this world. Probably I felt that there was monotony in a contented, harmonious married life, nothing to write about. It was only a broken marriage or one at a breaking-point that offered literary material. I had no facility for typing, and wrote everything in the best calligraphy I could manage, pinned the sheets neatly, wrapped them into a package, and carried them to the editor with no doubt that he would accept them with joy. My junior uncle, who was hardly at home but was in and out at certain specific hours for a wash or a change of dress, admonished me constantly, while passing, to write suitably and try and please the editor and forget all that damnfool stuff about Malgudi and such things. So one day I took the literary package to George Town and placed it before the editor. He offered me a seat, and glanced through the sheets. I had managed to fill about thirty or forty pages. After studying them, he said, 'You have a flair for writing, definitely, but you will have to understand our needs and aim at satisfying them. We should first take you as an apprentice in our office.' (Suddenly he had switched on to the royal 'we,' although I did not notice a second person in the establishment.) 'During the probationary period, you will not be paid. In fact we charge a fee, generally for training people. But in your case, I'll exempt you, being a nephew of my friend. I'll put you through every branch of the journal, and after three months, will consider paying you an honorarium commensurate with your aptitude.'

'What about these?'

'Of course we will use them as and when we find an opportunity after editing them suitably.'

'You will pay for them?' I asked timidly.

'Of course by and by, but not at present.' I didn't understand what he meant. All that I could gather was that he was looking for a free assistant, or probably an assistant blackmailer, as I found that he was proposing to subtitle his publication *True Tales* (of matrimony) and needed a researcher in social life.

*

I had to drop this man and look for other possibilities. I offered samples of my writing to every kind of editor and publisher in the city of Madras. The general criticism was that my stories lacked 'plot.' There was no appreciation of my literary values, and I had nothing else to offer. *Malgudi* was inescapable as the sky overhead. 'You have a command of the language, but . . .' was the almost routine statement made.

I stayed at Madras for three months during that year and pursued the editors of newspapers and magazines indefatigably. My junior uncle was at first wildly angry with me for letting down his matrimonial-gazette friend. But he still helped me to meet and talk to whomever he thought would be in my line, although most of them had only the English alphabet in common with me. Race-horse analysts, almanac-makers, film-writers, and so forth – most of them being my uncle's bar associates too. My senior uncle devoted most of his time to editing his literary weekly. He sat up all night in his attic (where I had once concealed myself) and wrote seventy-five per cent of the eight-page weekly himself under different pen names and in different styles, edited and rewrote other's contributions, corrected proofs, prepared copy, and studied voluminous ancient Tamil poetry. Also he conducted night schools for slum children, and left his desk for a couple of hours in the evenings on this mission. A hard-working intellectual who spurned the idea of earning money but somehow carried on. He had, of course, discarded his old hobby of photography; his cumbrous camera lay gathering dust on the top of a shelf, along with many other discarded things.

I showed him some of my writing. He read them and said, 'Good start, but you must study a lot more. Shakespeare, for instance, and above all *Ramayana* by Kamban. Try to read his version, and try to understand it with the help of the commentaries you will find in my journal. You will profit by it. Your writing will gain seriousness and weight. There is no hurry to seek publication yet. Keep writing, but also keep reading . . .' I could not quite accept his advice. I was setting out to be a modern story-writer, and he tried to make me spend my time poring over tough old classics. I listened to his suggestion out of politeness but rejected it mentally.

*

He wore himself out trying to establish his journal, and was on his deathbed in 1938 from a damaged heart, after running the weekly for eight years single-handed. I was in Mysore at the time and was summoned by a telegram to Madras to his bedside at the General Hospital. He lived for a couple of hours after my arrival, but had clarity of mind and speech. He gave me an advice with his last breath: 'Study Kamban's *Ramayana*.' I said, 'Yes, I will,' out of consideration, but with no conviction that I would or could ever be interested in Kamban; we were poles apart. I was a realistic fiction-writer in English, and Tamil language or literature was not my concern. My third novel, *The Dark Room*, was just out in London; and when I was leaving Mysore, the postman had handed me an envelope from my press-cutting agency containing all the first reviews, which were most enthusiastic. There was no reason why I should now perform a literary atavism by studying Tamil. So I rejected his advice as being the fancy of a dying man. Strangely enough, three decades later, this advice, having lain dormant, was heeded. I had totally forgotten my half-hearted promise, but in 1968 I became interested in Kamban, spent three years in reading his 10,500 stanzas, and found it such a delightful experience that I felt impelled to write a prose narrative of the *Ramayana* based on Kamban as a second volume to a work of Indian mythology. Strangely, I had completely forgotten the words of my uncle, until Marshall Best, my editor at the Viking Press in New York, asked just before I left for India if I had anyone in mind to whom I wished to dedicate the book. We had completed all the editorial work on my manuscript, and it was ready to be sent off to the printer. I suddenly recollected my uncle's injunction. I wrote out the dedication and handed it to Marshall at Kennedy Airport, where he had come to see me off.

My free-lance efforts at Madras bore fruit to the extent that I was given a book to review. Its title was *Development of Maritime Laws in 17th-Century England*. A most unattractive book, but I struggled through its pages and wrote a brief note on it, and though not paid for, it afforded me the thrill of seeing my words in print for the first time. The same journal also accepted a short story and paid ten rupees less money-order charges. My first year's income from writing was thus about nine rupees and twelve annas (about a dollar and a quarter). In the second year there was a slight improvement, as *The Hindu* took a story and sent me eighteen rupees (less money-order charges); in the year following, a children's story brought me thirty rupees. I handed this cheque to my father and he was delighted. He remarked, 'Your first and last cheque, I suppose!' I objected to his saying 'last' and he at once apologized. 'I don't know what made me say "last." Don't mind it.'

NINE

SIGHING OVER a pretty face and form seen on a balcony, or from across the street, or in a crowd, longing for love – in a social condition in which, at least in those days, boys and girls were segregated and one never spoke to anyone but a sister – I had to pass through a phase of impossible love-sickness. Perhaps the great quantity of fiction I read prepared my mind to fall in love with all and sundry – all one-sided, of course. Any girl who lifted her eyes and seemed to notice me became at once my sweetheart, till someone else took her place. Thus I had become devoted to a girl in a green sari with a pale oval face, passing down our street when we were living at Bojjanna Lines. She lived in the next street, the sister-in-law of an engineer, and I would have missed anything in the day rather than miss a glimpse of her. Sometimes I followed her quietly, like a slave, until she reached her gate and disappeared into her house without bestowing a single glance in my direction. I longed for some engineering business that might warrant a visit to her brother-in-law and then a gradual development of an acquaintance, the relationship maturing until I could freely propose to her, à la Victoria Cross or Marie Corelli. I was obsessed with her night and day, and I had no doubt that she would receive the impact of my thoughts, as Marie Corelli had taught me to believe that true love recognized no boundaries or barriers.

I lost sight of this girl suddenly – but found another, a little farther off, standing on the terrace of her home drying her hair – I noticed her at first on my way to the college, and then looked for her constantly on the way to and from; sure enough she would be there, a squat lumpy girl, but I loved her none the less. I think she was a flirt in her own way, ogling at every passer-by – not necessarily only me. I lost interest in her soon and bestowed it on another girl going to Maharani's College, who used to give me a smile and pass on. All this love for someone was necessarily one-sided and unspoken. But it made no difference. It gave me a feeling of enrichment and purpose. Among an inner circle of friends we always discussed girls and indulged in lewd jokes and enjoyed it all immensely. The blind urge to love went to fantastic lengths – I even fell in love with a lady doctor who had come to attend my mother because she spoke a few words to me whenever I greeted her; she was a British lady well past middle age, stout and married. But I saw great possibilities in her and read a significance in every glance. Love, especially one-sided, can know no bounds, physical, racial, of age, or distance. My most impossible infatuation was for a penfriend I had in England; we exchanged letters every week. She sent me her photograph and I sent her mine. I kept her photo in my breast pocket and hoped she did likewise with mine – five thousand miles away; even if I wished to reach her, it would mean a P&O voyage of four weeks. I wrote impassioned love-letters which she rejected outright; she wrote back impersonal letters describing a holiday in Brighton or her latest collection of stamps. Although she protested against the tone of my letters, she never stopped writing, and that seemed to me a hopeful sign. I continued to send her my unmitigated love in every letter, and treasured her cold, impersonal replies and the scent of her stationery for years – until I was married, when I threw them over the wall.

*

After the false starts, the real thing occurred. In July 1933, I had gone to Coimbatore, escorting my elder sister, and then stayed on in her house. There was no reason why I should ever hurry away from one place to another. I was a free-lance writer and I could work wherever I might be at a particular time. One day, I saw a girl drawing water from the street-tap and immediately fell in love with her. Of course, I could not talk to her. I learned later that she had not even noticed me passing and repassing in front of her while she waited to fill the brass vessels. I craved to get a clear, fixed, mental impression of her features, but I was handicapped by the time factor, as she would be available for staring at only until her vessels filled, when she would carry them off, and not come out again until the next water-filling time. I could not really stand and stare; whatever impression I had of her would be through a side-glance while passing the tap. I suffered from a continually melting vision. The only thing I was certain of was that I loved her, and I suffered the agonies of restraint imposed by the social conditions in which I lived. The tall headmaster, her father, was a friend of the family and often dropped in for a chat with the elders at home while on his way to the school, which was at a corner of our street. The headmaster, headmaster's daughter, and the school were all within geographical reach and hailing distance, but the restraint imposed by the social code created barriers. I attempted to overcome them by befriending the head-master. He was a book-lover and interested in literary matters, and we found many common subjects for talk. We got into the habit of meeting at his school after the school-hours and discussing the world, seated comfortably on a cool granite *pyol* in front of a little shrine of Ganesha in the school compound. One memorable evening, when the stars had come out, I interrupted some talk we were having on political matters to make a bold, blunt announce-ment of my affection for his daughter. He was taken aback, but did not show it. In answer to my proposal, he just turned to the god in the shrine and shut his eyes in a prayer. No one in our social condition could dare to proceed in the manner I had done. There were formalities to be observed, and any talk for a marriage proposal could proceed only between the elders of families. What I had done was unheard of. But the headmaster was sporting enough not to shut me up immediately. Our families were known to each other, and the class, community, and caste requirements were all right. He just said, 'If God wills it,' and left it at that. He also said, 'Marriages are made in Heaven, and who are we to say "Yes" or "No"?' After this he explained the difficulties. His wife and womenfolk at home were to be consulted, and my parents had to approve, and so on and so forth, and then the matching of horoscopes – this last became a great hurdle at the end. He came down to a practical level one day, by asking me what I proposed to do for a living. Luckily for me, at about that time a small piece that I had written ('How to Write an Indian Novel,' lampooning Western writers who visited India to gather material) had unexpectedly been accepted by *Punch* and brought me six guineas. This was my first prestige publication (the editor rejected everything I sent him subsequently) and it gave me a talking-point with my future father-in-law. I could draw a picture of my free-lance writing for London papers and magazines and explain to him that when my novel was finished it would bring in income all my life and fifty years after. He listened to me with apparent interest, without contradicting me, but off and on suggested, 'I'm sure, if your father used his influence, he could fix you in a government job at Bangalore. Won't he try?' This always upset me, and I immediately explained my economic philosophy: how I spurned the idea of earning more than was needed, which would be twenty rupees a month or, with a wife, forty rupees, and I expected my

afternoon. The play was called *The Home of Thunder* – a frightful tragedy in which all the principal characters are struck dead by lightning on a tower open to the skies, the play ending with a clap of thunder. It was a highly philosophical play examining the ideas of love, resignation, and death, the writing of which diverted my mind a great deal. I had great hopes for its future, and in due course sent it round to all kinds of producers and directors in every part of the civilized world. I had forgotten all about its existence till a few months ago, again when David Higham's office discovered and returned the manuscript while clearing out old papers.

The evil of my stars soon became a matter of discussion among the headmaster's astrological group. He sought me out and sent me here and there to meet his colleagues and talk it over with them and bring him their opinions and conclusions; finally he sent me along to meet an old man, living not far from us in the back of a coconut garden. His name was, strangely, 'Chellappa-sir,' I don't know why – perhaps he was a retired teacher – and he was said to be an expert. I went to his house and explained my mission. He snapped at me, 'What do you want me to do? Am I Brahma to change your stars?' He looked angry for some inexplicable reason. 'Go and tell that headmaster one thing. I don't care whether his daughter gets married or not; I'll hold on to my views. I have spoken to that man again and again, but still he is full of doubts. If he knows better astrology than I do, he should not trouble me like this. If he listens to reason, he should go ahead and fix a date for the wedding, that's all. I see no harm in it. He hasn't noticed the moon's position in his daughter's horoscope, which neutralizes the Mars. But that man expects me to give him a guarantee that Mars will not harm his daughter's life. I can give no such guarantee. I am not Brahma.' He raised his voice to a shrieking pitch and repeated, 'I do not care whether that man's daughter is married or not . . .'

In spite of all these fluctuations and hurdles, my marriage came off in a few months, celebrated with all the pomp, show, festivity, exchange of gifts, and the overcrowding, that my parents desired and expected.

Soon after my marriage, my father became bed-ridden with a paralytic stroke, and most of my mother's time was spent at his side upstairs. The new entrant into the family, my wife, Rajam, was her deputy downstairs, managing my three younger brothers, who were still at school, a cook in the kitchen, a general servant, and a gigantic black-and-white Great Dane acquired by my elder brother, who was a dog-lover. She kept an eye on the stores, replenishing the food-stuffs and guarding them from being squandered or stolen by the cook. Rajam was less than twenty, but managed the housekeeping expertly and earned my mother's praise. She got on excellently with my brothers. This was one advantage of a joint family system – one had plenty of company at home. Yet with all the group life, there was still enough privacy for me and my wife. We had a room for ourselves and when we retired into it, we were in an idyllic world of our own. Within six months, she proved such an adept at housekeeping that my mother left her in complete charge, and we found the time to exchange pleasantries and intimacies only when she took a little time off during the day and came to my room or at night after everyone had retired and the kitchen door was shut. Presently I did not find too much time to spend at home either.

In order to stabilize my income I became a newspaper reporter. My business would be to gather Mysore city news and send it daily to a newspaper published in Madras called *The Justice*. The daily was intended to promote the cause of the non-Brahmin who suffered from the domination of the minority Brahmin class in public life, government service, and education. Though *The Justice* was a propagandist paper against the Brahmin class, it somehow did not mind having me as its correspondent in Mysore. I left home at about nine in the morning and went out news-hunting through the bazaar and market-place – all on foot. I hung about law courts, police stations, and the municipal building, and tried to make up at least ten inches of news each day before lunchtime. I returned home at one o'clock, bolted down a lunch, sat down at my typewriter, and typed the news items with appropriate headings. I now had an old Remington portable (the double-barrelled one having been given away for twenty rupees, off-setting the bill for cigarettes and sweets at a shop), which was a present from my younger sister. It took me an hour or more to type the items, and then I signed and sealed the report in an envelope, and rushed it to the Chamarajapuram post office before the postal clearance at 2:20 p.m. If my youngest brother (Laxman, now a famous cartoonist) was available, he would be ready, with one foot on the pedal of his bicycle, to ride off to the post office for a tiny fee of a copper for each trip; but when he wasn't there, I practically sprinted along with my press copy. There was really no need to rush like that since most of the news items could wait or need not be published at all; but we were in a competitive society: I feared that other Madras papers like *The Mail* or *The Hindu*, whose correspondents had telephone and telegraph facilities, might get ahead of me. But those correspondents were lofty and did not care for the items I valued.

After the despatch of the copy, I relaxed in my room; that was also the time when my wife could give me her company. I described to her the day's events, such as traffic accidents, suicides, or crimes, which were the grist for my mill; then I sank into a siesta for an hour and was ready to go out again at four o'clock after a cup of coffee. This time it would be a visit to the magistrate's court before closing time, to take down the judgement in a counterfeit case or murder conspiracy. On Saturday afternoons I sat at the municipal meeting, watching the city fathers wrangle over their obscure issues – all through the evening it would go on. In those days there were always a couple of lawyers on the council, and they never permitted the business to proceed beyond an examination of the procedure and the by-laws. No more than a couple of items in the voluminous agenda would be covered at the end of two hours. After a coffee break, I would suddenly clutch the agenda papers and leave, afflicted with a headache. Some days there would be academic matters to cover, a distinguished visitor lecturing at the university or a senate meeting. In those days there was a local League of Nations Union, which strove to establish peace in this world in its own way. The secretary of this union, who was a history professor, decreed that our reports should be scrutinized by him before we filed them. I resisted his order as an encroachment on the freedom of the press, and he threatened to discredit me as a correspondent (which would, in effect, only mean denying luncheon facilities) whereupon I declared that I would report him to our Journalists' Association, pass a resolution against him, and syndicate it to all the world's press and denounce him as an autocrat and enemy of freedom. He said, 'Do you know that I have powers to smash you and your papers . . .' I walked out of the union meeting in protest, and so did a couple of my colleagues. I began to ignore its activities and boycotted its functions. I realized soon that this did not affect the prospect of world peace either way, nor provoke my news-editor to question why I was not covering the League of Nations Union.

Murders were my stand-by. From Nanjangud or Chamarajnagar, at the extreme south of Mysore District, the police brought in a steady stream of murder cases. On such occasions, I let myself go. I hung about the mortuary for the post-mortem verdict and the first police report. As long as I used the expression 'alleged' liberally, there was no danger of being hauled up for false reporting or contempt of court. I knew a lot of police officers, plain-clothes-men, and informers – apart from presidents and secretaries of various public bodies (including the Pinjarapole, a home for aged or disabled animals) who craved publicity and sought my favour. Quite a number of wedding invitations came to me from fond parents hoping for a report and a photograph of the bridal pair in the paper. I should have gladly given all the space available to whoever wanted it, but my news-editor, when he did not reject it outright, mutilated and decimated my copy. He compressed my most eloquent descriptions into two lines. What did I make out of it all? Our contract was that I would be paid three rupees and eight annas per column of twenty-one inches. I fancied that the news I sent would cover at least fifteen inches each day and fetch me at least seventy-five rupees a month, but thanks to the news-editor's talent for abridgement, I had to crawl up each day by fractions of an inch. I measured my total 'inchage' with a scale at the end of the month and sent my bill; and they would invariably doubt and disallow my measurements and send me some arbitrary amount, never more than thirty rupees, often less.

But I enjoyed this occupation, as I came in close contact with a variety of men and their activities, which was educative. It lasted for about one year, and might have gone on, perhaps indefinitely, but for a letter I sent to the editor, which soured our relationship. They had withheld my payment for three months, and I wrote to say, 'I am a writer in contact with many newspapers and periodicals in America and England, who make their payments on precise dates; I am not used to delays in payments . . .' To which the editor replied, 'If you are eminent as you claim to be, you should not mind a slight delay on our part; if, on the other hand, you could realize that after all you are a correspondent eking out your income with such contributions as we chose to publish, your tone is unwarranted by your circumstances.' I resented the tone of their reply, and decided to give up this work as soon as I could afford it.

Money was a big worry. When a cheque was delayed, it caused all kinds of embarrassments for me. My budget was precisely framed. I had to find money to pay for my share of the expenses at home, also for face powder or soap that my wife would ask for. I grandly promised her even a sari, and bought her a green one on credit costing about sixty rupees, the shopman agreeing to take instalments of ten rupees on the fourth of every month. If I delayed, a bill-collector would appear on the morning of the sixth at our gate, demanding the instalment. He was a tall, gaunt man, with sunken cheeks and the expressionless face of a corpse. When I heard the clicking of the gate latch, I would tell myself, 'Here it cometh, my lord,' echoing Hamlet. I rushed forward to stop him before my wife or anyone else could see him, and turned him back with soft words, promises, and a small tip for coffee; until I liquidated this debt, I felt guilty whenever I saw my wife in the green sari, as if I had given her a stolen present.

I continued to send in my reports of the turbulent city of Mysore, and off and on received a cheque from *The Justice*. But I voluntarily stopped this work on the day I received a cable from my friend Purna, who was now at Oxford: 'Novel taken. Graham Greene responsible.' My friend and neighbour Purna, who used to hop over the wall and come to listen to my reading of *Swami and Friends*, had left in August 1931 for Oxford, promising to find a publisher for my book while he was there. When I had completed the novel, I faithfully despatched it to Allen and Unwin and when it was returned, to another publisher and then another. I had got used to getting back my manuscript with unfailing regularity once every six weeks – two weeks onward journey, two weeks sojourn on a publisher's desk, and two weeks homeward journey with a rejection slip pinned to it; all in all it provided me with six weeks of hope! I had got used to this as an almost mechanical process and had shed all emotions surrounding a rejection. The last publisher to return it to me was Dent, and I had advised them in my covering letter to forward the manuscript when rejected to Purna at Exeter College, Oxford. I sent a parallel letter to Purna advising him to weight the manuscript with a stone and drown it in the Thames. Purna, however, seems to have spent much of his time visiting London and carrying the manuscript from publisher to publisher. After trying them all, he wrote to me, 'To the Thames? No need to hurry. May be never. Do not despair.' This went on while I was spinning out measurable news for *The Justice*. Graham Greene was living in Oxford at that time. Purna, by some instinct, approached him and gave him my manuscript. An introduction thus begun established a personal interest and a friendship between us that continues to this day. Graham Greene recommended my novel to Hamish Hamilton, who accepted it immediately.

Purna's cable made me gasp with joy and surprise. I saw myself in a new role as a novelist. I could see the relief in my wife's face, although she did not want to be too demonstrative about it. The first thing I did on receiving the cable was to write to *The Justice* that I would not be able to supply them any more news from Mysore, although the advance from the novel was twenty pounds (less fifty per cent tax).

Swami and Friends was published in the October of 1935. A few reviews were enthusiastic, but it had no sales; it appeared in the company of record-breaking best-sellers such as *Man the Unknown* and *Inside Europe*, and was simply flushed out of sight in the deluge. So much so that Hamish Hamilton rejected his option on my next novel, *The Bachelor of Arts*, with the words, '*Swami and Friends* was a sad failure. I don't think *Chandran [The*

Bachelor of Arts] is going to do any better. I hope someone will prove me wrong some day.' Twenty years later I met Hamish Hamilton in London at a party in the office of the *Spectator*, where Graham Greene had taken me. It was a very interesting and cordial meeting. Egged on by Greene, Hamilton remembered his comments on my literary future, joked at his own expense, and then remarked, 'Remember, I was your first publisher, and I always feel happy at the thought of it.' Next morning he sent me a copy of his *Majority*, which has extracts to celebrate thirty years of his publishing firm, generously inscribed for me.

Thanks again to Graham Greene's recommendation, *The Bachelor of Arts* was published by Nelson, fulfilling a fancy I had entertained several years before when a Nelson representative had come from Edinburgh to see my father about the supply of books for our high-school library. I had confided to this salesman, 'If I write a book, will you ask your company to publish it?' 'Undoubtedly,' he had said and given me his card.

*

Change after February 1937. My father lived up to the last date of the month, as if to satisfy a technical need, and died leaving us to draw his pension for the full month. That was all the resources we were left with. My father had never believed in savings, property, and such things.

Now we feared a total economic collapse. But we managed. My elder brother, now back from Madras, as an experiment had opened a small shop in a new extension and called it National Provision Stores. Seenu had a government job and moved off to Bangalore. Mine was still a pure gamble. Sometimes I wished that I had not given up *The Justice*, but I was sustained by the gambler's inexhaustible hope and a Micawberish anticipation of something turning up. With a second novel published and a daughter added to the family, life seemed to be not so bad. Short stories were being accepted in India as well as abroad – Graham Greene helping me in London. So after all my claim to the editor of *The Justice* about contacts with London editors was being fulfilled, although it had, perhaps, been premature. The great gods who could view the past, present, and future as one bloc would have realized I had not been false!

My brother and I shared the household expenses. He looked after the supplies and miscellaneous items of expenditure, and I had to see that the house rent was paid; all aspects of shelter were to be my responsibility. 'Rama Vilas,' in which we lived, was to be retained at any cost; there could be no question of our moving to another house. Fortunately our house-owner lived in Bangalore and only came down to Mysore once a month to collect the rent. I told him once, 'The rent is my responsibility. I have no fixed income. If my books sell, the royalty will come in only in December and June. So please permit me to settle the rent once every six months, although I will pay into your bank account whatever amount I'm able to earn meanwhile.' He was good enough to accept this arrangement. Now I had a scrappy, fitful income from various sources. In addition to other items I had to find money for baby-food, gripe-water, and toys. I did a variety of writing: humorous article every week for a *Merry Magazine* at ten rupees a week; a most taxing experience for me – to perform a thousand-word literary clowning week after week. I had also begun my third novel, *The Dark Room*. I took a pad and pen and disappeared every morning for three hours. I found it impossible to write at home now – there were far too many worrying distractions, and also the baby. She was just a little over a year old, and I found it impossible to remain at my desk when she was around, since my wife often left her in my care while she was busy in the kitchen or in the garden gathering flowers for my mother's daily worship. I had also a routine duty to carry my daughter to let her watch the pink bougainvillaea flowers over the compound wall of Reverend Sawday's bungalow at the corner. She would gaze at the bunch of flowers for about ten minutes with rapt attention, and then I would have to lift her up to give her a glimpse of a white terrier that barked and frisked about inside the Reverend's compound. Only then would I be free to deposit her at home and leave.

Before sending me out, my wife would give me a cup of coffee and sometimes whisper a warning: 'Don't make a fuss. Not enough coffee powder at home. Get some at the store when you return.' I set out to do my writing at the College Union, where the secretary had given me a room. I shut myself in for three hours, gazed on the green football field outside, across the street, and spun out the fate of Savitri – the heroine of *The Dark Room*. I was somehow obsessed with a philosophy of Woman as opposed to Man, her constant oppressor. This must have been an early testament of the 'Women's Lib' movement. Man assigned her a secondary place and kept her there with such subtlety and cunning that she herself began to lose all notion of her independence, her individuality, stature, and strength. A wife in an orthodox milieu of Indian society was an ideal victim of such circumstances. My novel dealt with her, with this philosophy broadly in the background. I wrote nearly a thousand words before I went back home for lunch, exhausted, but also feeling triumphant at having done my quota of work for the day.

The Dark Room, once again read and approved by Graham Greene, was published by Macmillan in 1938. I had the unique experience of having a new publisher for each book. One book, one publisher – and then perhaps he said to himself, 'Hands off this writer.' Hamish Hamilton, then Nelson, now Macmillan.

TEN

MACMILLAN had produced *The Dark Room* attractively. The reviews were favourable. I was buoyed up by them but my wife did not share my optimism. She preferred to await the royalty statement, and when it did arrive, it revealed an 'Unearned Advance' (the advance was £40 less tax) rather than a cheque. I dashed off a letter to Macmillan suggesting that they should have made the existence of the book better known to the public. Their depots in India had no copies, and the literary pages of newspapers and magazines carried no advertisements. I had naïvely expected the publishers to seize upon the reviews and splash the quotes all over. Macmillan replied that they had advertised the book as best they could under the circumstances (what did it mean?). Their message typed in purple copying ink, and pressed out, possibly, on a wet sheet of paper, looked jittery and cheerless.

Presently, I had to set aside my principles and settle down to hackwork. At this time my friend Purna, who had introduced my *Swami and Friends* to Graham Greene at Oxford, was on the personal staff of Sir Mirza Ismail, the dewan (Prime Minister) of Mysore, and was in touch with the 'state guests' coming to Mysore. At this time Mr. Somerset Maugham was staying in one of the Maharaja's mansions. He was attended on by the Maharaja's private secretary, Sir Charles Todhunter, an encrusted British administrator who had made it his mission in life to keep Indians properly occupied and out of mischief. It was his belief that what the Indian urgently needed was not political freedom but social graces. With this aim, he patronized Child Welfare, the Society for Prevention of Cruelty to Animals, the Good-Manners League, and other innocuous institutions calculated to wean away the natives from mischief. The names Gandhi or Nehru were taboo in his presence. Sir Charles believed that, properly handled, Indians could shape into useful citizens, as proved by the terrified and efficient clerks he had in his establishment. My brother Seenu was one of them, having been spotted by Sir Charles at Bangalore and roped in. While Sir Charles kept his dogs, cats, and ducks sheltered in the main building, he housed his clerks in a derelict unventilated barnyard, under a smoky, verminous tile roof, at the farthest corner of the compound, and summoned them to his presence with a buzzer. He glared at them over his narrow spectacles, thumped his huge fist on the desk, and drove them to slave for him twelve hours a day by sheer bullying. His main job was to see that the Maharaja did not lose his loyalty to the British Crown or establish any industry which might affect British interests. To question this man on literary matters would seem incongruous at any time. Yet Somerset Maugham seems to have done so. At a banquet arranged in his honour (although I cannot believe that either the Maharaja or his private secretary would have seen a novel by Maugham or anyone) Maugham asked, 'How is it that I haven't seen anywhere the famous writer living in this city – Narayan?'

Sir Charles turned to his assistant in consternation. 'Find out if there is a famous writer in Mysore. Consult the university vice-chancellor, if necessary.'

After due investigation Maugham was told, 'There is no novelist in Mysore. We may, however, find you one in Bangalore' (at a safe distance of one hundred miles). The honoured guest looked displeased and declared that his entire trip now seemed to him a waste.

Although I don't fully believe this story (imagined by someone and passed on from person to person), I suspect that Purna may have asked Somerset Maugham on some occasion, 'Have you read *The Dark Room*?'

'I shall look for it in London when I go back.'

'Would you like to meet Narayan?'

'I am afraid there is no time now, but do give him my compliments.' (Later Maugham read *The Dark Room* and did write to me.)

Then Purna may have told this story to someone, with a slight exaggeration, and, passing the round in official circles, it developed into a full-fledged apocrypha and eventually reached Sir Mirza Ismail's ears. Sir Mirza, perhaps not wishing to share Todhunter's reputation, invited me to meet him at his Mysore residence, called 'Lake View,' overlooking Kukanahalli Tank. This was an unexpected offshoot of Maugham's visit.

As if to substantiate my theory that fiction outlasts fact, the original story is still current after nearly forty years! Occasionally I come across some ancient raconteur retailing his own version: 'It seems P. G. Wodehouse when he came to Mysore, as a state guest, demanded to meet R. K. Narayan and lost his temper when Todhunter said there was no such person in the city! And he left in a huff, declaring that he could not accept the hospitality of such an ignorant host.' Or sometimes another name may be substituted for Maugham's: H. G. Wells, Bernard Shaw, or John Gunther.

Sir Mirza's call made me extremely uncomfortable. I had got on so far without meeting a minister or a Maharaja, and I hated the very idea. I did not even possess the right dress for visiting a dewan. A dhoti and a cotton jacket over it were my main outfit, and I had resisted the Western style of dressing for many years.

My normal wear was stylish enough for my encounters along Sayyaji Rao Road. Nowadays, young people, hippies and non-hippies alike, have accustomed us to indifferent clothes and styles, but those were times when any doorman would turn you back if you were not properly dressed. I attempted to back out of this engagement, but Purna would not hear of it. He almost bound, gagged, and dragged me on, to the presence of Sir Mirza, tutoring me all along the way on how to impress him. 'Don't fail to explain how the Indo-Saracenic tradition seems to be continued in the present-day buildings of Mysore, of course tempered and modified by contemporary needs.' He came up to the threshold of Sir Mirza's chamber talking in whispers. I heard him say, 'Also explain how the Chamundi Hill presiding over this city reminds one of the ancient Greek cities.' Sir Mirza loved Mysore City, had remodelled its buildings, boulevards, and avenues, and liked to hear a good word about it. I walked into his room in my dhoti, cotton coat, and a muffler around my neck, feeling uneasy, as if I had gone wrapped in a bath towel. In contrast to me, he was impeccably dressed in a silk suit and a black fur cap. He offered me a seat and put me at ease, enquiring about my literary activities in a general way without going into details. My prepared speech beginning, 'The Indo-Saracenic . . . et cetera,' was in a mess, delivered piecemeal, in irrelevant fragments, whenever a pause occurred in Sir Mirza's own speech. He was too polished to show any surprise, but gently assured me in the course of our conversation that if I wished to join the publicity department he would take me in. I declined the offer and expressed only a wish to write on Mysore.

Purna innocently believed that any magazine or newspaper editor in India would commission me to write on the Indo-Saracenic theme if ordered by Sir Mirza, who lost no time in writing his proposal to several editors, who, in their turn, politely welcomed his suggestion (Mysore government being the biggest advertisers of sandalwood soap and silk), but when approached put me off unceremoniously.

Finally, the government of Mysore commissioned me to write a travel book on Mysore. I was given a railway-pass for travelling within the state, a cash advance for expenses, and letters of introduction to various district officials asking them to give me 'all facilities.' Mysore State, extending up to Bombay in the north, Madras in the south-east, and Kerala in the south, offered inexhaustible material for a travel-writer, being rich in rivers, mountain ranges, forests, and wild life, not to mention temples, monuments, and battle-scarred fortresses and ruins. By bus and train, I explored every nook and corner, listened attentively to the claims of the local enthusiast in any obscure mountain retreat or village lost in a bamboo jungle that here was to be found the earliest sculpture or civilization or the highest waterfall in the world, or that those footprints on a forest track were Rama's, or that the golden tint to that lily pond was imparted by Sita when she plunged in for a cool bath. In every place everyone found token of a legendary hero or a mark left by the gods during a brief sojourn. Belur and Halebid temples, with their twelfth-century carvings, or the dungeons of Srirangapatnam, where in the seventeenth century Tippu Sultan had kept his British prisoners, seemed modern in comparison. I climbed a peak of the Western Ghat to view the Arabian Sea coast, visible as a vibrant string of silver far off. And also I went down eight thousand feet underground to see a gold mine in Kolar, where the heat and pressure choked one's breath out. I accomplished the full range of travel, leaving my wife and child back in Mysore City, and all through racked with anxiety for their welfare. Now and then, I found an excuse to cut short my tour programme and return home unexpectedly to satisfy myself that all was well. I did somehow get through it all in the end, came back to Mysore with an accumulation of notes and data, and settled down to write my book. I was supposed to make good use of gazetteers and blue books, but I found such reference work tedious and impossible, with the result that though my legendary tales and descriptions might beguile, the factual portions turned out to be unreliable. A friend in the Mysore Civil Service, who knew all parts of the state, marked in red the inaccuracies in my manuscript, and declared that the book should be kept away from any unwary traveller setting out to see the state. I believe I tried to save myself by appending 'about' or 'approximately' before every date or distance; with all that, I don't think my book has seriously misguided anyone.

When the manuscript was ready, the dewan ordered the government press to print an edition under my direct supervision: paper, type, and binding to be chosen by me. The superintendent of the press seemed overwhelmed by the authority vested in me and became so attentive whenever I opened my mouth to say something that I found it embarrassing. It was becoming a difficult situation for me, since I knew nothing about the printing of books, but those who placed me in control of the government press must have assumed that an author of three novels published in England must, of course, be an expert in printing. Every afternoon, sitting there as an advisor to the superintendent, I had to manage a difficult conversation across his table.

'Do you approve of these types – Plantin twelve point or Baskerville ten point?' placing specimens reverently before me.

I looked at them casually and said, 'Well . . . this one seems passable . . .'

'Shall I order the matrices for this series?'

'Surely, go ahead, but you must see that they don't delay . . .' I had to advise, approve, and at the same time learn what on earth it was all about.

'These are samples of binding cloth. Walthamstow is the best of course, but we shall order whatever you choose, and this is thirty-six-pound featherweight paper . . .'

I looked through the offerings gravely, disapproved a few on principle, and approved others. I also threw in a hint. 'Let us keep as close to the get-up of *The Dark Room* as possible; the dewan liked it.'

At once the superintendent secured a copy of *The Dark Room* and went at it with measuring scale, callipers, and magnifying glass, after stripping off its jacket, binding, and spine. Cables were sent to England to ship the materials immediately. Not a moment to lose. No one paused to consider if there was any need for all this desperate rush. However, working at fever pitch, the press was able to deliver one thousand copies of my *Mysore* within six weeks.

I carried the first copy to Bangalore and presented it to the dewan at his office in the red secretariat. I had thought that my financial troubles were now at an end. Not only the writing of the book but the production of it in convincing form struck me as an achievement, although it was a responsibility undertaken ahead of experience. Sir Mirza glanced through a couple of pages of the book and murmured a thanks. He extended his hand across the table, and said, 'Thank you again, it was good of you . . .' which seemed to mean now 'Be off, young man, I have so much to do now . . .' I was aghast. I had expected a cheque to be held out to me rather than a bare hand. When I left home I had budgeted so many items for the 1,200 rupees I was to get. I had asked my wife, 'Do you want anything from Bangalore?' She was more realistic. 'Let us first see the cash, and then we will decide how to spend it' – whereupon I had lost my temper and cried, 'Always doubting! So much like your dear father!' She immediately protested. 'Why talk of my father now?'

'Why not?' I cried wildly, and added, 'I have discussed it all with Purna, and he has spoken to the dewan. Twelve hundred is not a big sum. Some foreign journalists demanded ten times that for the same proposition, but the dewan was keen on giving it to an Indian writer, and that is that.'

She would not share my optimism, and it angered me and led to arguments when I left. I promised my daughter when she followed me up to the gate, 'If you are good I will get you . . .'

Now in the dewan's office I respectfully stood up and said, 'Yes, sir, thank you. May I know when I may expect payment?'

'Oh!' he exclaimed, suppressing his astonishment at a writer's sullying his thoughts with monetary notions. 'What do you expect?'

'Twelve hundred,' I said. Purna had advised me to be specific while mentioning a figure.

'Very well,' said the dewan. 'As you go down, see the chief secretary and tell him. He will help you.'

I walked into the chief secretary's room with assurance. He was busy over the telephone and looked through me without either welcome or rejection. I stood at the edge of his table and, when he put down the telephone, proclaimed, 'The dewan has sent me to see you.' I explained my mission.

He motioned me to a chair and asked, 'Is there any paper about your demand? Did the dewan give you anything in writing?'

While I was wondering how best to answer, the chief secretary lost track of my case owing to the interruptions caused by the telephone, visitors, and his factotums bringing in papers. After an hour he looked at me again and said, 'Please give a written requisition, otherwise we won't be able to proceed.'

He pushed across a sheet of paper on which I wrote, 'As promised by the dewan, I shall be glad to accept . . . et cetera . . .'

The chief secretary studied my paper. 'Did the dewan actually promise or promise to consider?'

I did not understand the subtle distinction, and merely said, 'He promised that you would arrange the payment. Please make it urgent as I would like to go back to Mysore this evening.'

'Yes, yes, of course, by all means; you may go if you like, and you will hear from us in due course.'

He apparently dismissed me from his thoughts, but I stuck to my seat in the hope that he might still produce a cheque somehow. He left at lunchtime without any further word. I followed him out and asked, 'Should I see you again?'

'Why not?' he replied vaguely, and was off. (I never saw him again, neither that afternoon, nor next day nor ever in my lifetime; he was always away or at a meeting and could not be approached.)

After waiting all that afternoon I thought that I might see Sir Mirza again and complain of his order not being carried out, but when I reached his office, I found the door shut. I was told that the dewan had left for a conference at Simla, a thousand miles away. I sought out Purna. He merely said, 'Don't worry,' and sent me on to see the publicity officer next morning, explaining, 'Your payment will have to come only from the publicity department.' I sat all day in front of the publicity officer. Attendants were fetching stacks of paper and dumping them on his table. He rummaged through them every time only to say, 'Your file has not yet come . . .'

'Where from?' I asked.

'From the finance section.'

At six o'clock my papers arrived. By then I was exhausted watching the traffic of people and papers across his room. The publicity officer glanced through my file and pushed it across for my edification. My recent application was on top of a pile of letters, its margin marked in a variety of inks and handwritings, and all the preceding correspondence between me and the government were below. I read with a sort of poignant interest the marginal notes on my application for payment. 'Financially unacceptable,' the finance department had said. Someone had queried, 'Was there a contract?' It was answered by the legal section, 'None. Government's commitment limited to providing facilities for writing the book, vide D.O. dated . . .' A further query was, 'Were quotations invited from other authors? What was the basis on which this particular author was selected for this commission?' I could not resist adding, on the marginal space available, my own reply to this particular question: 'A bogus story arising from Mr. Somerset Maugham's visit. You may ask if you please who was Somerset Maugham and if his name is also in the approved list of contractors.'

We cannot console ourselves with the thought that this happened three and a half decades ago. Bureaucracy is the same even today the world over. If I should make the mistake of accepting a government commission to write a book today, I am sure it would go through the same process of elucidation and final liquidation through self-defeating procedures.

ELEVEN

IN JANUARY 1939 my wife went to her parents' home at Coimbatore for a holiday. It suited me, for the time being, since I had to be away too on business. Mysore was an excellent place to write in, but Madras was my market; I spent a month there and succeeded in selling the Tamil rights of *The Dark Room* to a serial publication, and managed a few other sales too. But the real achievement was a contract with *The Hindu* to write a sketch or a story every week for their Sunday columns, at the rate of thirty rupees apiece. I had also agreed to write features and talks for the All India Radio, and odd items for a film studio, such as scraps of dialogue scenes and 'treatment' for the harebrained conceptions fancied by a film producer. When these arrangements were completed, I returned to Mysore.

Now, I found life at home impossible without my wife and child around, and tried to spend my time outside. Leaving early in the morning, I sauntered down Vani Vilas Road, at old Agrahar slowed my steps in order to pray briefly to Ganesha installed under a peepul tree on the roadside; the scent of jasmine sold on the footpath, and of sandalwood from manufacturers of incense sticks in the neighbourhood, wafted in the air. Sometimes I was trapped by the frying smell emanating from a little restaurant tucked away in a lane off the main road, where I ate a *dosai*, washed it down with coffee, and, lighting a cigarette, resumed my walk. I was careful with money, never spending more than a rupee a day. All morning I wandered. At every turn I found a character fit to go into a story. While walking, ideas were conceived and developed, or sometimes lost through the interludes on the way. One could not traverse the main artery of Mysore, Sayyaji Rao Road, without stopping every few steps to talk to a friend. Mysore is not only reminiscent of an old Greek city in its physical features, but the habits of its citizens are also very Hellenic. Vital issues, including philosophical and political analyses, were examined and settled by people (at least in those days) on the promenades of Mysore. You came across long-lost faces and stopped to enquire what had happened between then and now. If Socrates or Plato were alive, he would have felt at home in Sayyaji Rao Road and carried on his dialogues at the statue square. Apart from such profound encounters, it was also possible that you would run into a man who owed you money or the plumber who had been dodging you, or you could even block your lawyer's path for a consultation. With such interruptions it was possible that ideas got scattered and the thread of a story got lost. However, I generally kept my subject in mind and, returning home, sat at my desk and wrote till the evening. On Wednesdays I had to mail my story for *The Hindu*. The ideal I had in mind was to write and work on it well in advance, and post it smoothly on Wednesday; but it never worked out that way. A touch of desperation to catch the deadline seemed to be an important element in the final shaping of a story. Invariably I was engaged till the last possible minute in working on it, and then I had to carry the packet to the railway station almost at a run, and shove it into the mail van. It had to reach the editor's table on Thursday morning, when the Sunday page was to be made up.

My working programme was disrupted on any day I realized that my wife had not written a letter on the due date. She always gave me her solemn word that she would drop me a note at least once a week to say that she and the child were keeping well, but she could never keep this promise. I generally expected her letter on Monday afternoon, allowed a couple of days' margin, and felt anxious if there was still no letter on Wednesday. No reason for this state, as I was fully aware that she was not a letter-writing sort. At the beginning of our married life, when we were occasionally separated, a few blue note-papers passed between us, and if I delayed an acknowledgement, she would again write to me in a tone of grave anxiety; but nowadays she had become too casual, and kept me on tenterhooks. I would constantly be on the point of sending off a telegram to say, 'How are you? Why no letter?' But she was opposed to the extravagance of a telegram. Once or twice when I did send one she resented it as being too dramatic, and embarrassing before her brothers and sisters. I had to content myself with urgent importuning letters, also threatening to send a telegram if she defaulted. Ultimately she would write and lighten my mind for at least another week, but no longer than a week. On another Wednesday the problem would start all over again, somehow exactly on the day when my story should be in the mail. I have always found story-writing and letter-writing incompatible. I don't know how other writers feel about it, but I find it easier to write a story than a letter, and if I am bogged down in letters, I become desperate for fear that I may miss my day's schedule. On Wednesdays, I also attempted to draft a brief note or telegram, and as a consequence floundered in my composition for *The Hindu*. If the editor of *The Hindu* sometimes found my story difficult to pass, the responsibility must be traced to the missing letter from Coimbatore. Now, looking back, it seems absurd to have placed so much value on exchange of letters. We were not newly-weds to need constant reiteration of mutual love, nor was there any occasion for letters, as the absence of any news

her at the railway station and immediately my daughter ran forward and clung to my arms. I took them home in a tonga. All the way, in the carriage as we drove along, Rajam narrated the events that had taken place at Coimbatore on the eve of her departure. 'My father was not too happy to let me go even last evening.'

'Oh – impossible man!' I cried.

'Just as we were leaving, our house-owner, you know that fat man, came in with some demand. My father lost his temper, and then the man shouted wildly, "Vacate my house immediately." Just as they were arguing, a black scorpion fell from the roof-tile where I stood, and I narrowly escaped being bitten. My father felt that these were inauspicious signs and wanted me to postpone my journey.'

'Oh, no,' I said. 'That would have been impossible. Your father seems to be quarrelsome!'

'But you see me here, why blame him at all? I'd not have delayed my return. You seem to fret so much. I only stayed back for my sister's sake. I am happy I could see her – that was all.'

Within a hundred days of her arrival, Rajam had departed from this world. She caught typhoid in early May and collapsed in the first week of June 1939. Looking back it seems as if she had had a premonition of her end, and had wanted to stay back with her parents and sister. I have described this part of my experience of her sickness and death in *The English Teacher* so fully that I do not, and perhaps cannot, go over it again. More than any other book, *The English Teacher* is autobiographical in content, very little part of it being fiction. The 'English teacher' of the novel, Krishna, is a fictional character in the fictional city of Malgudi; but he goes through the same experience I had gone through, and he calls his wife Susila, and the child is Leela instead of Hema. The toll that typhoid took and all the desolation that followed, with a child to look after, and the psychic adjustments, are based on my own experience. That book falls in two parts – one is domestic life and the other half is 'spiritual.' Many readers have gone through the first half with interest and the second half with bewilderment and even resentment, perhaps feeling that they have been baited with the domestic picture into tragedy, death, and nebulous, impossible speculations. The dedication of the book to the memory of my wife should to some extent give the reader a clue that the book may not be all fiction; still, most readers resist, naturally, as one always does, the transition from life to death and beyond.

The loss of my wife was sudden and not even remotely antici-pated by me – although my father-in-law had had his doubts while looking into my horoscope earlier. But now I had to accept her death as a fact. One had to get used to the idea of death, even while living. If you have to accept life, you are inevitably committed to the notion of death also. And yet one cannot stop living, acting, working, planning – some instinct drives one on. Perhaps death may not be the end of everything as it seems – personality may have other structures and other planes of existence, and the decay of the physical body through disease or senility may mean nothing more than a change of vehicle. This outlook may be unscientific, but it helped me survive the death of my wife – though I had missed her so badly while she was away at Coimbatore. I could somehow manage to live after her death and, eventually, also attain a philosophical understanding.

But it was not easily attained. The course was full of hardship, doubts, and despair against a perpetual, unrelenting climate of loneliness. I never hoped that I could ever take any more interest in the business of living, much less in writing. But it was Graham Greene who said in his letter of condolence, ' . . . I don't suppose you will write for months, but eventually you will.' A hope corroborated by another friend, a mystic, Dr. Paul Brunton (to whom I shall refer again), who said one night at the end of an after-dinner walk, 'You will write a book which is within you, all ready now, and it is bound to come out sooner or later, when you give yourself a chance to write.' These remarks I accepted without contradiction, but I felt clearly within my mind that I would never write a word again in my life. I had lost my anchorage. There was no meaning in existence. Dismal emptiness stretched before me. There were a hundred mementoes and reminders each day that were deeply tormenting. I could not bear to stay in the room I had once shared with my wife. I slept in the hall. I tried to cut away from every little reminder, but the scent of Dettol and of burnt margosa leaf permeated the walls and haunted me night and day. (The fumes of margosa, in addition to Dettol, were supposed to destroy all infection.) I found it impossible to wake up in the morning and get through the daily routine of washing, eating, clothing, and so on. I suffered from a horrible numbness. My mother and brothers felt distressed at the manner in which I was slipping down. I avoided company. Late in the evening I sallied out for a walk, smoked a few cigarettes, avoided all friends, and came back in time to put my daughter to sleep. I had to give her a great deal of my company in order to make up for her mother's absence. She slept in a bed next to mine in the hall, and had adapted herself to the change in a most handsome manner. She never asked questions. Her uncles and grandmother at home were devoted to her, looked after her, and diverted her mind with visits to the zoo, shops, and movies; plenty of toys came to her by every mail. We kept the door of her mother's room permanently closed. On the actual day of the funeral, the child had been sent away to the zoo early, before she could notice anything.

She had been trained to keep away from her mother's room since the day the fever had been diagnosed as typhoid. And now, more than ever, she was not supposed to go near that door. Yet two weeks later, the child gleefully confided to me, 'I know she is not there. I pushed the door, it opened, and I peeped in.'

'They have taken her to the hospital,' I explained lamely.

She was just three years old, but displayed a considerateness which was precocious. She never questioned me or anyone about her mother again.

More painful than the bereavement was the suggestion from well-meaning but foolish men that I should remarry sooner or later. When someone spoke thus, I spat fire at them. I had had a Tamil pandit at college who met me at the market-place and said, 'Lost your wife? How dreadful! You must remarry soon. When old clothes are gone, you have to buy new ones. When she has left you without a thought, why should you care?' He spoke as if my wife had deserted me. Many searing retorts welled up within me, but I suppressed them. A lawyer in our street peeped over our gate to say, 'Sorry, mister. I have also suffered the same fate. You must and will get over it.' He had lost four wives in his matrimonial career and remarried each time, but at the moment was again a widower. 'Your solution does not seem to have worked in your case,' I wanted to say, but again swallowed my remarks.

My sister at Madras suggested that I should go over there for a change of atmosphere and spend some days at her house, where my daughter could have the company of her children. Everyone urged me to go away from Mysore, from oppressive surroundings and reminders. So, one afternoon, I packed a trunk with our clothes and set off for Madras by the afternoon mail.

The need to keep up an appearance of cheerfulness and interest in living helped me a great deal. I had to amuse the child so that she might not turn round and suddenly demand her mother's attention. She enjoyed the train journey and later was lost in the company of other children at Madras. Plenty of toys, dolls, playmates, and games – she was happy. In a few days, she had got into the routine of her aunt's home on Cathedral Road, and did not see much of me. At night, when she felt sleepy, she needed to be put to bed by me; at other times she left me very much alone.

My sister had given me a room in her house, and I kept myself to it very much. I tried to read a little. I tried to resume my writing for *The Hindu*. There was a beach at the eastern end of Cathedral Road, and I managed to spend a long time each day walking through the sands and along the surf for a mile or two towards Santhome and back; the bright sun and blue sea in the evening, the stars and phosphorescent waves, the far-off lights of steamers on the horizon at night, the cool waves lapping up to the knee (I walked barefoot, tucking up my dhoti) – all this pulled me, so to speak, out of a shell of memories and speculations. When I ploughed my way back home through the sands, I felt tranquil. Every little experience at such moments heightened and refined my perceptions. Gradually, memories of funerals and details of the sick-room began to fade and in their place I tried to catch and retain the moments of elation I felt at the touch, sight, and sound of the sea.

Walking was my only occupation. I had no friends. I was not interested in movies, and I found all books tedious. I could walk endlessly, morning and evening. I found walking a great help; while one foot follows another, with a minimum watchfulness to avoid the traffic, one's mind becomes more passive and receptive and acquires a rhythm in which one's thoughts, philosophy, and conclusions get properly sorted out. I must have walked several miles each day. My ideas were changing and becoming clarified. I still could not bring myself to the point of writing. I was confirmed in my mind that I would not write any more. None of the elements that would normally stimulate one to write was there – no curiosity, no interest in people or my surroundings, no desire for achievement of any sort, or for a future, which seemed relevant only to the extent that it involved the child.

*

One evening while returning home from the beach, a cousin of mine whom I had lost sight of long before, who worked in an import firm in George Town, accosted me at a street crossing and expressed his condolence, which I accepted mutely, and we stood there not knowing what to say further. He added, 'I wanted to write to you, but somehow put it off . . .' I listened with indifference. During the recent months I had been the recipient of so many sympathetic remarks that I was beginning to accept them with a professional casualness. I could listen to an hour's sympathetic address stonily, without saying a word in reply. Depending upon the age of the speaker, I could sense what was coming: a hint – or blatant advice – to remarry, or rally oneself, grit one's teeth, steep oneself in work, and so forth. The talk went on the expected lines, and as I was about to say 'Thanks, good-bye,' and turn away, he said something that held me. 'I have a friend, Raghunatha Rao, have you met him? You will find him interesting. He lives nearby, come with me. He is an interesting man.' At first I resisted his suggestion, but he was insistent and I yielded. I had nothing much to do one way or another. Dinner time was only at nine o'clock at my sister's house, and my daughter would not look for me until after her cousins had gone to bed.

This street-corner encounter, though it looked so casual, led on to contacts and experiences which profoundly affected my future, and saved me from disintegration.

Raghunatha Rao lived in a little house in Mylapore, in a private road, behind the Royapetta tramline, under the shade of a coconut grove; so peaceful that one could hardly imagine that only one hundred yards away tram wheels screeched and ground the face of the earth. Mr. Rao was a robust-looking man, in his early forties perhaps, full of gusto and good cheer. He received us at the top step of his veranda, explaining, 'You will excuse me for staying where I am. I like to ascend or descend as little as possible.' He took me in and introduced me to his wife in an inner room – a pale, slender person, extremely gentle in speech and movement. He introduced me as the author whose stories they liked – they particularly remembered two or three ghost stories that had appeared in *The Hindu*. His rippling good humour seemed contagious, and I stayed with him for an hour joking and laughing. Evidently my cousin must have hinted to him of my loss, and after coffee and conversation when we parted, he said, 'Why don't you come on Wednesday evening about six o'clock? We are conducting some psychic experiments and you may find them interesting.'

I was not sure that I wanted any of it. So I said, 'Thanks. I'll come if I am free,' and left it at that.

My cousin, who accompanied me, said, 'Nice chap, he is interested in all sorts of things. He has suddenly got this new interest; and I make fun of his latest hobby, but he has a sense of humour. He is a lawyer, you know; but he is rich and doesn't have to practise very much, and can afford to indulge his interests, mostly religious. Both husband and wife are alike.' He bade me good-night and added, 'You may go any time you like to Rao, and you will like his company; don't go if you don't like to, on Wednesday.'

On Wednesday, I debated within myself if I should meet Rao or not; I had no faith in spiritualism, which seemed to oversimplify the whole problem of life and death with its trappings and lingo. In any case, on Wednesday I started out for the beach without any definite plan in mind, and on an impulse turned along the tramline and on to Rao's house. He was happy and seated me in the hall and engaged himself in casual talk. At about six-thirty his wife came in and said, 'Ready.'

'Put another chair for our friend, he may want to watch, would you like to come in?'

They took me into a small chamber, with curtains drawn. A small round table with sheets of paper and a dozen pencils mended were kept on it. He showed me a chair, and sat opposite to me. His wife sat to his right. Before settling down he said, 'We are only trying and experimenting – I have no definite views on this subject. I am generally sceptical, but when I was writing down something, some months ago, I felt that my hand was being forced by some other power, and I let it go, and there came out of it certain writing, which interested us. And so, at the same hour on the same day, we sit and try and certain scribblings occur, which sometimes turn out to be prayers or hymns. We have been going through this for several weeks now. When I sit up alone, nothing happens. But when my wife sits along with me, a lot of writing comes through. When we get a third person in, sometimes everything stops and the visitor will generally go away after making fun of us. But the presence of some persons who are psychically inclined may prove helpful. I wonder what your company is going to mean to us today . . . Let us see.'

'What do you want me to do?'

'Nothing. You just sit there and watch and don't say anything when my hand starts writing . . . Only keep an open mind. Don't obstruct with negative thoughts. After all, only thirty minutes by the watch . . .'

During those thirty minutes, he held the pencil over the sheet of paper and it moved and filled the pages in large letters. 'Your band of helpers are here, and welcome your visitor today. We are aware that he has suffered a recent bereavement, lost a person he loved. We can see that his heart is still very heavy and anguished.

If we could help him, and others like him, to understand the nature of life and death, and relieve the pain at heart, we will have achieved our purpose. Death is only the vanishing point of the physical framework in which a personality is cast and functions; that same personality is unperceived before a conception, and will be lost sight of again at death, which we repeat is a vanishing point and not the end . . .' Thus it went on sheet after sheet, at a pace of writing which was not normal – the pencil points broke off or tore through the paper. At one stage, the pencil said, 'The lady is here, but will not communicate with her husband directly yet. By and by, perhaps, when she is calmer. She is somewhat agitated today, since this is her first effort to communicate with her husband. She is disturbed by the grief of her husband. We on this side are directly affected by the thoughts emanating in your plane, and do our best to set your minds at peace. Today, she feels happy that there is an opening created and she could make some effort to influence your thoughts . . . The lady wants to assure you that she exists but in a different state, she wants you to lighten your mind too, and not to let gloom weigh you down. She says, now you are told I am here; by and by when you have attuned your-self, you will feel without proof or argument that I am at your side and that will transform your outlook. She advises you not to let anxiety develop about the child. She is well, and she will grow up well. I watch her. I now see her in a room, wearing a blue skirt, and playing with another child; they have three dolls between them. The lady says good-bye until next week.'

Thirty minutes were over, and twenty-four hundred words had been written, which is an extraordinary speed of writing. If you could write by hand five thousand words an hour, a novel of eighty thousand words should be completed in sixteen hours! As a professional writer, I ought to envy anyone who can drive a pen at this speed! Rao himself was surprised, and confessed, 'Don't you imagine that this is my normal writing. It takes me a whole hour to fill the back of a postcard, and then I am stuck for ideas after the second line . . . That's the reason why I'm reluctant to answer letters and thus have lost the goodwill of many relatives and friends.'

Apart from the actual details of paper, pencil, and speed, I began to sense Rajam's presence at that table. What she is supposed to have said or Rao's pencil wrote was secondary. The actual presence felt at this sitting in the stillness and dimness of that little room had a profound effect on me. When I went home that evening, I felt lighter at heart. I remember there was a quarter moon in the sky – its light seemed deeper and more subtle than ever – the air seemed bracing – everything looked subtler and richer. When I went back to my room, the child, I noticed, was poring over a picture book, hardly looking up to note my arrival. I was happy to be ignored. I did not stop to verify what the colour of her dress was – whether blue or some other colour, whether she had been playing with three dolls or two at the time. All that factual side seemed to me immaterial. Even if Mr. Rao had had his own sources of enquiry and was dashing off the information at the sitting, even if Rao caught telepathically whatever went on in my or anyone else's mind, it did not matter to me. Even if the whole thing was a grand fraud, it would not matter. What was important was the sensing of the presence in that room, which transformed my outlook. The medium, after all, was a human being, his mind and his writing could be subject to many shortcomings and trickeries, both conscious and unconscious. But I still valued the experience for its final effect on me. All through the week I looked forward to the next meeting. On Wednesday, I was there again at Rao's house. And then again. Of course, much of the writing was of doubtful value or could even be rejected as sheer nonsense. At the same time there came through flashes of unquestionable evidence – such as reference to a piece of jewellery in a box of whose existence I was not aware, some incident or remarks at her brother's house which could be verified. Although I felt indifferent about such research during her communications, she urged me to follow them up, and I pursued them for her sake. I came across surprising facts that way. Sometimes, unasked, she would give an answer to some personal problems passing in my mind on my way to Rao's house. But, at first, I treated them as possible telepathic readings by Mr. Rao himself – some details would be startling, such as where I thought of such and such questions, and who was with me at that time. Even if all that were only Rao's telepathic competence, it still seemed to me extraordinary. Telepathy? Well, what if? How did it reduce the value of the experience? Apart from it all, what really mattered to me ultimately was the specific directions that she gave step by step in order to help me attain clarity of mind and receptivity.

My next three months' stay in Madras was worthwhile – not from a professional point of view, but for my own development. In course of time, my wife was able to communicate directly at Mr. Rao's sittings. Week after week, she gave me lessons on how to prepare myself so as to be able to communicate my thoughts or receive hers without an intermediary. At the thirty-minute sitting, she criticized my performance in the preceding week. 'It is no use, your sitting up with such rigid concentration: that's just what I do not want. I want you to relax your mind; try to make your mind passive; you can think of me without desperation and also make your mind passive . . . no, no, it's not the rigour of a yogi's meditation that I suggest; this is a more difficult thing, create a channel of communication and wait. Keep your mind inactive . . . I can see that you still worry too much about the child . . . Take good care of her, but don't cramp her with so much anxious thought, which has grown into a habit with you . . .

Two nights ago, when you were about to fall asleep, your mind once again wandered off to the sick-bed scenes and the day you mourned my passing over . . . No harm in your remembering those times, but at the root there is still a rawness and that interferes with your perception. Until you can think of me without pain, you will not succeed in your attempts. Train your mind properly and you will know that I am at your side. Not more than ten minutes at a time should you continue the attempt; longer than that, it is likely to harm your health . . . Take care of yourself . . . I am watching the child, and often times she knows I'm there, but she won't talk to you about it . . . She may sometimes take it to be a dream . . . For instance, the other night, you remember a wedding procession that passed down your road, you were all at the gate to watch it, leaving her asleep in your room . . . I approached her at that moment; if you had ever questioned her next morning, what she dreamt, she would have told you point blank, 'I dreamt of Raji . . .' Sometimes she may not remember, often she will not care to talk . . . Children are much more cautious than you think . . . Children are precociously cautious. After coming over, I have learnt so much more about the human mind, whose working I can directly perceive . . . In your plane, your handicap is the density of the matter in which you are encased. Here we exist in a more refined state, in a different medium . . . I wish I could explain all that I see, think, and feel . . . When you are prepared for it, I'll be able to tell you much . . .'

In these twelve weeks, a voluminous quantity of paper had grown out of the sittings, which Mr. Rao gave me when I took my daughter back to Mysore. I never met him again. We corresponded for a few months. We tried remote sittings – that is, on a certain day and hour I sat alone, a couple of hundred miles away at Mysore or Coimbatore, and linked to Rao mentally, and he sent me the writing that resulted from this effort. After some time even that amount of dependence on the medium became unnecessary. I felt able to manage for myself independently, since psychic experience seemed to have become a part of my normal life and thought. In a few months I became an adept. That psychically I had developed became evident in course of time. One night, during a subsequent visit to Madras at my sister's house, I heard strange tappings on the window-pane, repeated exactly at a particular spot, at twelve-thirty in the night, which continued for ten minutes, ceased, and were repeated intermittently until two a.m. My sister was scared; she switched on the lights and shut herself in another part of the house; but I drew up a chair and watched the window-pane. Although I felt slightly nervous, I was determined to sit through and understand the message. At five a.m. the telephone rang to tell us of the passing of a close relative (of whom we were very fond) exactly at twelve-thirty in the night when the tapping had started.

I could catch telepathic messages or transmit my thoughts to others; and I could generally sense what was coming ahead or anticipate what someone would say. On another occasion, I was again at Madras, spending a night at a friend's house in Nungambakkam. I saw a ghost enter my room when I had just gone to bed and was not yet asleep. I heard the latch rattle, and I looked at the door, saw the ghost glide in, go past my bed, take a couple of turns in the room, and vanish. I felt a sudden chill in the air . . . But for it, it might have been just someone coming in to pick up matches . . . I didn't feel frightened but only slightly shaken and found it difficult to compose myself to go to sleep again.

Following the directions given, I practised psychic contacts regularly for some years, almost every night. I found it possible to abstract myself from my physical body (a process taught by Paul Brunton) and experience a strange sense of deliverance. And then gradually the interest diminished when I began to feel satisfied that I had attained an understanding of life and death.

Thereafter I resumed my normal life and activities. I wrote my fourth novel. That was *The English Teacher*, published in 1944 by Eyre and Spottiswoode, where Graham Greene was now a director. The Second World War was raging, and paper shortage and all kinds of shortages had disrupted the publishing world, but Greene managed to find the quota of paper for an edition of 3,800 copies, and the book has been in print ever since.

Out of all this experience a view of personality or self or soul developed which has remained with me ever since. 'Now we know in part, then fully, face to face . . .' said St. Paul; our faculties are limited by 'now' and 'here.' The full view of a personality would extend from the infant curled up in the womb and before it, and beyond it, and ahead of it, into infinity. Our normal view is limited to a physical perception in a condition restricted in time, like the flashing of a torchlight on a spot, the rest of the area being in darkness. If one could have a total view of oneself and others, one would see all in their full stature, through all the stages of evolution and growth, ranging from childhood to old age, in this life, the next one, and the previous ones.

Somehow, for the working out of some destiny, birth in the physical world seems to be important; all sexual impulses and the apparatus of sexual functions seem relevant only as a means to an end – all the dynamism, power, and the beauty of sex, have a meaning only in relation to its purpose. This may not sound an appropriate philosophy in modern culture, where sex is a 'fetish' in the literal sense, to be propitiated, worshipped, and meditated upon as an end in itself; where it is exploited in all its variations and deviations by movie-makers, dramatists, and writers, while they attempt to provide continuous titillation, leading to a continuous pursuit of sexual pleasure – which, somehow, Nature has designed to be short-lived, for all the fuss made – so that one is driven to seek further titillation and sexual activity in a futile never-ending cycle.

*

Paul Brunton, who came to India to study Indian philosophy and mysticism, stayed in Mysore for two years in order to complete a book he was writing. He had taken a house in Vontikoppal, at the northern section of the city, a couple of miles from my house. One or two evenings in the week, I took a walk to his place, and dined with him. His dinner invariably consisted of a boiled potato, a slice of bread, and a cup of yoghurt. He abstained from meat and alcohol, and found this diet appropriate for his life of meditation and yogic practices. We had kindred interests. When he had arrived from Egypt he had just published a book, *A Search in Secret Egypt*, which I had reviewed for *The Hindu* in sceptical and tongue-in-cheek style. But when I met him, I found him to be a genuine person. I found that many of his experiences, which had sounded improbable, were true. He had spent midnights in the chambers of Pyramids and had had strange psychic encounters and visions. Under the guidance of certain practitioners of the esoteric arts in Egypt, he had attained mastery over deadly serpents, scorpions, and wild animals, the power to view the past and future, and various miraculous and magical powers* of not much value in one's evolution. A sixteenth-century Tamil mystic had sung, 'One may learn to walk on water, mesmerize a mad elephant, muzzle a tiger or a lion, walk on fire, and perform other feats, but yet the real feat would be to still the restless mind and understand

---

* Known as *Siddhis* in Sanskrit. There are eight of them, such as walking on fire and water, ability to transmute, to attain invisibility and all kinds of controls over the elements.

one's real self.' Every spiritual seeker acquires at some stage occult powers but ultimately gives them up as being unessential. Paul Brunton abandoned all his earlier practices when he came to Mysore, and, having had the guidance of Ramana, a savant who resided in Thiruvannamalai Hills, he meditated on the question 'Who am I?' The enquiry 'Who am I?,' he explained, eliminated the self-conscious framework limiting one's personality, and one attained a great spiritual release. When we met, we exchanged our experiences, analysed and evaluated them. Off and on he would disappear for a few months, going in search of some mystic in the Himalayas, and would return as suddenly to Mysore.

*

By about 1942 our home was richer by the addition of two sisters-in-law, both my elder and my younger brothers being now married, the latter having a son, too. Our house had become full and lively. My sisters-in-law relieved my mother of a lot of housekeeping duties, and also practically adopted my daughter, who went to a school in the mornings but spent the rest of the day in the company of her aunts. I was left very much alone to go about my searches and researches. But she expected me home at nine in the evening, and felt uneasy if I stayed out late. When that happened she would be watching at the window, slightly red-eyed. At such times my mother would chide me, 'Have some thought for the child and come home early. She has some curious misgivings if you are not home early.'

TWELVE

THE DISRUPTION caused by the Second World War had its repercussions in my career too. We suffered black-out, food rationing, alarums and excursions even in our distant corner of Mysore, but in addition to what the public suffered, I had my own personal losses to count. My agent, David Higham, now perhaps a major general, was away on army duty. The British publishers were nowhere to be seen, all copies of my books, waiting to be sold, were destroyed in a London blitz, and the little royalties trickling in half-yearly were gone. *The Hindu* could not take in as many contributions as it used to owing to newsprint shortage, printing-ink shortage, and god knew what else. It was necessary for me to do something else to keep myself going. No way left for a writer to reach a public. Journalists and writers who could get into the propaganda organization were saved, but I was outside such activity. Neither politics nor the war were of any interest to me. *The Hindu* provided a little space for my contributions, but I was getting tired of recording my observations of the life around. The constant state of receptivity and then the eight-hundred-word expression thereof were becoming tiresome – I wanted to put an end to this activity before the readers of *The Hindu* should also begin to think likewise. I had written at this period mainly on the difficulties of the common man – how he had to stand in a queue morning after morning, at the ration shop, bus stand, and cloth shop, unfamiliar with the devious paths to the black market, and struggling through life in his effort at maintaining himself and his family. It had no doubt a relevance to the days we lived in, but I felt tired of this and similar themes. A time came when I could not bear to put pen to paper or go through anything I wrote in manuscript or print. Nor could this weekly grind leave me any time or energy to plan major writing. Every sentence that I wrote seemed to be taking me away from something more important. I was racked with a feeling that I ought to be doing something else.

Our meeting-ground nowadays was a doctor's shop on Hundred Feet Road. It was called Narashimha Pharmacy and was presided over by our family doctor, who was an all-rounder — interested in tennis, cricket, and politics. He attended on my daughter and kept her in good health. It was my habit to drop in at about seven in the evening to report to him on our welfare generally or to ask if some tonic should be continued. The business part of the visit was secondary, as he had provided several rows of chairs facing his table and enjoyed company. My friends gathered there every evening, and we sat around and discussed life and literature. During one of those sessions, I cannot say whose idea it was, but the idea was born that I should start a publication of my own. I rejected the proposal for obvious reasons. Purna, who used to float in and out of this group constantly, suggested puckishly, 'Why not call it "Indian Thoughtless"?'

'Let us call it "Indian Thought," which will amount to the same thing,' said another.

It was agreed that this was a good title. We began to talk out the details. It was to be a quarterly publication devoted to literature, philosophy, and culture. The doctor promised to get all his sick clients to subscribe for the journal. Purna again promised government patronage in the form of advertisements and library orders.

Another friend promised to write the accounts. My own business would be to gather material and see that it was printed.

I could hardly sleep that night. My head buzzed with plans and calculations. The first thing I did on the following morning was to compose a manifesto to be circulated widely, announcing the inception of the journal. I shut myself in my room after persuading my daughter to go to the neighbour's house and play with their children. I did not want to be interrupted while performing editorial tasks. I packed into the manifesto all my ambition: to phrase our culture properly; to utilize the English language as a medium for presenting our cultural heritage – Indian classics and philosophy from Sanskrit and a score of other regional languages, modern writing included; and to encourage original English writing of the highest quality. My ambition could properly have been realized if I had had planned a cultural encyclopaedia of five thousand pages, but within the dimensions we had set, one hundred and twenty pages once a quarter, it would have seemed madness to try it, more like packing an elephant in a demy-octavo carton. I wrote numerous letters each day to possible contributors and well-wishers, the letter always beginning pompously: 'Now I am writing to you as the editor of a literary quarterly, whose scope the enclosed pamphlet will explain. I should indeed be delighted to consider . . . and I can offer a small honorarium of thirty rupees per article . . .' My tone suggested that the editorial rank had been thrust on me by a vast, stubborn committee; there was nothing to indicate that it was a self-imposed honour. I felt I had all along missed my true vocation, which was to be an editor. I remembered J. C. Squire and other editors of my 'Divine Music' days, and decided that I would not be like them. I was destined to discover and nurture a whole school of young writers. If I were to reject an article, I'd write a letter more in sorrow than in arrogance, and never send a printed rejection slip under any circumstance. Being an editor, I could be sure of finding a place for my own writing. (I realized in due course that it was more profitable to sell my pieces to other magazines.)

I had one hundred rupees in the bank and that had to be the starting capital. Mr. Sampath, who was my printer (and who became a character in one novel and two film stories), had said bluntly, 'I'll do the printing side but you must provide the paper. I can't invest on that now. I should not have normally minded this service, but the present time is bad for me. I am ordering a double-cylinder printing machine and possibly a colour-printing Heidelberg – all my capital is locked up. You will be happy when you see your cover printed on Heidelberg and your text printed sixteen pages at a time.' After all this he asked for an advance. With a subscription of twenty-five rupees each from the more affluent four among my friends and one hundred of my own, I paid an advance to the printer, and expected the first number to come out in a week. Actually it took three months for the first one hundred and twenty pages to be printed, for although Sampath held forth visions of sixteen pages at a time, he could print only four on a treadle. It took me several weeks of anxious trips to the press before the last forme could be printed. After I had given up in despair, Sampath knocked on my door one midnight, and there he stood on the veranda holding out to me dramatically the first copy of *Indian Thought* and a thousand more waiting to be unloaded from a tonga at the gate. He looked triumphant as he said, 'They are all neatly wrapped up; all that you have to do will be to write the addresses and send them off – if matter for the next issue is ready, I'd like to start it right away – my machines cannot remain idle, they are now geared for your job – you have no idea how many jobs I have had to turn down . . .'

Indian Thought overwhelmed and frightened me – it had an orange wrapper with my name on it, with a spreading banyan tree and a full moon behind silhouetting a tramp lounging in its shade. I turned the pages and hoped my readers would find them edifying and illuminating. My own piece was some scrappy anecdote of one page, and right on the second page started a paper on 'Probability,' a highly technical exposition in mathematics. I had to include it because it was the first paper to arrive when Sampath was clamouring to compose the first forme. It was included also because its author was a revered mathematics teacher who had helped me to pass a public examination. I could not refuse when he offered it for publication, but it made no sense to me. Page after page of speculation and a formula on heads and tails of a tossed coin – HTTHH or something like that. I had a hope that my readers might understand it better, but literally only one reader congratulated me on my discovery of this paper. All the others ignored it or wrote to me in exasperation. A humorous story called 'Unveiling' translated into English from an Indian language, which I later discovered was only a P. G. Wodehouse story in an Indian garb. Somebody's travels in Ladakh, an economic theory, a review by Paul Brunton of some mystic poems which baffled my understanding – an absolute hotchpotch, justifying the original title suggested by Purna, 'Indian Thoughtless.' I brightened the second number with a deliberate effort – abandoned the orange cover with its silhouette of a tramp, and gave it some less ascetic appearance; included jokes and *obiter dicta* at page ends as space fillers. I soon realized that the fillers read better than the stuff occupying the main space on a page. What the journal was in my anticipation was a readable light magazine, every page alive with style and life, profundity with a light touch. What it actually turned out to be was a hotchpotch of heavy-weight academics and Wodehouse rehash – the sort of journal I would normally avoid.

*

I was soon to realize that the basis of my selection of articles for *Indian Thought* was not sound and in one instance even dishonest. I came to this conclusion when I read through in print a story of a mad dog living on filth. This dog had been a human being, a youth, in the previous incarnation, as narrated by the dog itself in the first person. The youth married, but went to bed with his newly-wed wife without going through a proper nuptial ceremony, and when discovered in the act felt guilty and committed suicide; was reborn as a street mongrel; one summer day in the heat of the sun, allayed his thirst by lapping up gutter water; went stark mad, attacked passers-by, and was clubbed to death. The story had a peculiar, pointless savagery which struck me as uproarious. It had been given to me by my newest landlord (the previous owner being dead), a young man who was setting out to be a writer, among other things. He did not approve of the half-yearly rental arrangement I had made with his predecessor, but demanded a monthly settlement, also an increase. The attack on Pearl Harbor and a mild air attack on Madras had created an exodus to the inland safety of Mysore. As a result, there was pressure on housing, and landlords generally tried to dislodge their existing tenants under various pretexts. My landlord also had caught the general trend, and began to drop in frequently from Bangalore to suggest that we vacate the house, ostensibly to enable him to carry out major repairs and modification. It was unthinkable at this stage. Our family had nowhere else to go, and we could not afford the latest scales of rent, even if we had found another suitable house. I was beginning to be haunted by visions of our family carrying rolls of bedding and trunks, trooping along the streets of Mysore, with the Great Dane on a leash, coming to rest in the open veranda of Sita Vilas Choultry – a public rest-house on Hundred Feet Road, where travellers and homeless persons congregated. This was a dreadful prospect to contemplate. My elder brother somehow would not take our landlord's demands seriously. He just said, 'No one can disturb us, don't worry. Let us offer the young man a little increase of rent and we will be safe.' We offered a rise of ten rupees, which our landlord accepted; he left us in peace for a couple of months, but turned up again with the same story of having to remodel the house. I was the only one available to him for such discussions, my elder brother being away at his fertilizer factory morning till night, and my younger stuck in the palace office all day. The young man would drop in, take a seat, and start a discussion on houses in general and the problems of maintenance, always concluding, 'We are obliged to remodel this house in the quickest time possible as we are anxious to move in here from Bangalore; we don't feel that Bangalore is going to be safe any more with the Japanese planes coming up to Madras.'

I said, 'Why, there is every chance of their coming to Mysore if they come as far as Bangalore, after all such a short distance!' He changed his tactics presently, and explained that he was starting an Epsom salt factory in Mysore, was expecting war contracts, and wanted his house urgently. We had lived in this house for many years now, and it seemed impossible to move out of it at the present time. While I was wondering how to placate this young man and gain time, during one of his visitations he took out of his pocket his story and began to read it to me. I was struck by the sheer insanity of the whole conception and swallowing my judgement said some complimentary things about it. He looked pleased and for once went away without any mention of his house, and there was no more pleasing sight for me than his receding brown-suited figure (he was always dressed in a full brown suit without tie). I felt happy to have sent him away so pleased.

But I hadn't suspected the danger lurking in this situation. When the brown suit slid into my study next time, about two weeks later, he produced from his pocket a typed copy of his story, at a moment when I was struggling to make up pages to meet Sampath's demands. Sampath was becoming aggressive in regard to deadlines. He would keep sending me notes to say, 'We are waiting to finish your formes before fulfilling other printing orders. We request you to co-operate with us and not put us to a loss or blame us later if we take up other work and are thus forced to delay yours.' This man, genial and informal in person, always sounded forbidding in correspondence, with his first-person plural. When I was in this predicament with Sampath's messenger waiting at the door, the young landlord begged, 'I will be so happy if you can print this story somewhere.' I didn't want to lose a chance to place this boy under an obligation, and said point blank, 'If you are so anxious to see your story in print, give it to me in writing that you will not disturb us at least for two years more, and there is your chance to see your story in print. Otherwise you may take it where you please.'

'Two years undisturbed . . . ! Impossible!' he cried and left in a huff. I felt that this was the end, and that we should gird ourselves for moving to Sita Vilas Choultry. That night the brown suit appeared again at my door. He looked careworn and as harried as myself. I asked coldly what his business was. As I had hardened myself for the migration to the public charity home, I felt I could at least have the pleasure of talking in the tone of my choice. He looked cowed by my manner and said, 'Mr. Narayan, we are old friends. Let us compromise. Let us make it one year instead of two.' And I accepted his story, edited it, tried to make it sound less insane than it really was, and packed it off to the printer. When I read the story in the third number in cold print, I felt ashamed of myself as an editor; I felt I had prostituted my position for a domestic cause, and that my readers would be justified in stoning me at sight.

The fourth-quarter issue for October–November–December

1942 appeared in May 1943. Sampath, having had to print urgently an annual statement of a co-operative society and a Golden Jubilee Souvenir and twenty other items, had set aside my magazine. But he would not accept the blame for the delay. He said that I did not get him paper supplies in time, although lately he had assured me not to bother about such details any more as he had his own sources of supply. It had all become so nerve-racking that I decided to put an end to the publication with the fourth number. The journal had been financially self-supporting, but I felt that it was too much of a preoccupation and would kill me as a writer. My junior uncle, who was now a prosperous car dealer at Madras with many hundreds of clients eating out of his hand, had proved a dextrous salesman for *Indian Thought* too. Every day he had been sending a dozen addresses of new subscribers. He recruited all sorts of persons into our fold; people who would never turn the leaves of a book were now made to pay for the highbrow journal issuing from Mysore. I think my uncle must have offered them a drink and forced them each to part with a year's subscription. I had nearly a thousand subscribers on my list when I, or rather Sampath, decided to end the career of this journal.

Now I felt lighter at heart. No more worries about paper, printing, contributors, or subscribers. But it did not mean that my connection with the press had ended. I found Sampath a charming friend, always cheerful, bouncing with enthusiasm, full of plans (although not for printing jobs), and involved in a score of tasks not always concerning him. He specialized in the theatre, was a master of the dramatic arts, his office walls were covered with photographs of Sampath in various costumes and make-up and poses. He rehearsed his actors in his office, while galley proofs streamed down his desk untouched; he helped people in litigation by introducing them to his brother, an eminent lawyer; he found houses for those who needed that kind of help;

THIRTEEN

AFTER I HAD closed down *Indian Thought* and point blank refused to look at anything he wrote, my young landlord became aggressive. So every morning I went out to search for a house. It was a difficult task, as our requirements were rather complicated – separate rooms for three brothers, their families, and a mother; also for Sheba, our huge Great Dane, who had to have a place outside the house to have her meat cooked, without the fumes from the meat pot polluting our strictly vegetarian atmosphere; a place for our old servant too, who was the only one who could go out and get the mutton and cook it. We had all these conveniences at Rama Vilas, and we looked for a replica in every house we searched. Every day the pressure from the young landlord was increasing; apparently he had now come to live in Mysore. He would stroll around our garden proprietorially, look up at the coconut trees and count and recount the nuts, just to emphasize his ownership. We watched him through the window without any agitation, although legally we were entitled to this produce. Coconuts were a small price to pay for the benefit of having a roof over our heads. I avoided him. Finally it came to the point that he addressed me by mail with a registered letter, demanding that I vacate the house within fifteen days.

My brother as ever remained unperturbed. 'What if there is a notice? It is not so easy to throw out a tenant. We have been here for fourteen years, and any court will have to take that into consideration. They will have to concede us as least half a month for each year we have stayed, that way we will get at least seven months . . .'

I don't know where he got this piece of law from. However, I was worried; and so every morning, I made it a mission to search for a suitable house, and I also contacted some housing brokers. I went about, street by street, looking for TO LET signs. We were determined that we should not move too far out of our present orbit. Our milk-suppliers, children's schools, friends, contacts, and grocers were all here, and it would have been impossible to uproot ourselves completely and go out farther than Weavers Lines, Chamundi Extension, or Chamarajapuram. I examined at least two houses each day; houses became an obsession with me night and day. I felt it was degrading to live in a rented house and immediately applied to the City Trust Board for land.

Meanwhile, my landlord sent me another legal notice giving me ten days to vacate the house. I became desperate and went up to consult my friend Sampath as to what I should do now. He at once took me up a staircase to his brother's law office and succinctly presented my case to him. His brother was a busy lawyer, a mighty-looking man whose very personality was reassuring. He looked through my papers and said, 'I will deal with your landlord. Don't worry.' However, my mother insisted that I should not take advantage of the legal position but give up the house and move elsewhere. I continued my search.

On my rounds one morning when I was passing down the third street from ours, I saw Professor Hiriyanna, a venerable man who taught Sanskrit and Indian philosophy at the university, standing at his gate, and I stopped by for a chat. Although he was very much my senior, we often met at his gate or a street corner and discussed books and publishers. He was negotiating with

Allen and Unwin for the publication of his book on Indian philosophy, and felt confused by certain clauses in the publisher's contract and consulted me about their meaning. This morning, while talking on general matters, I told him also about my housing worries.

'Why don't you take that house?' he said, pointing at a big bungalow to his right. 'It is my daughter's, I think it is vacant. Rent and other details you will have to settle with her.'

It was a propitious moment. Within a week, we moved over to 963, Laxmipuram, only two streets away from our original habitat. It was a large house with a spacious compound, several rooms, and enough space for all of us and Sheba – above all the same neighbourhood as before.

*

In 1948, on the penultimate day of January, I plunged into house-building activities by turning the clod ceremoniously with a pickaxe on a plot of land allotted to me at Yadavagiri, situated on the northern outskirts of Mysore. The place was still undeveloped, but it was a highland giving a noble view over the landscape for miles around. We had selected this particular spot because of a frangipani tree standing on its edge in full bloom. In spite of the several aesthetic points in its favour, the place was desolate – miles away from where we lived, without a road, water supply, or electricity. The 'foundation' ceremony was conducted with gusto and bonhomie, with distribution of sweets and puffed rice under the frangipani, organized expertly by the contractor, who with a measuring tape and white paint ran around marking the foundation lines. It was all very convincing and filled us with hope and visions.

But that was the best part of the business. After such a spectacular start the house made only limping progress for the next five years – for want of funds, cement, steel, timber, and above all because of constant friction between me and the building contractor, who kept up a perpetual demand for money without showing commensurate progress in the building. I managed to find the money by borrowing. Payments produced only a short-lived friendliness, for he would turn up again with fresh demands. He had an extraordinary system of drawing his bills, adding up a criss-cross of measurements, rates, and charges and producing a total figure before which whatever money I gave seemed a trifle and left him grumbling. 'Unless I am paid for my work, I can't really go on.' Whereupon I'd borrow again and try to propitiate him. It took a long time for me to realize the fact that his system of billing was of a visionary nature, much of the demand being for impalpable, unseen items, and that I ought to get rid of him. The house made no visible progress but my debts were mounting, and shuttling between Laxmipuram and Yadavagiri on foot, sometimes two trips in a day, to supervise construction had exhausted my strength and wrecked my nerves. Once again with the help of Sampath's lawyer brother, I had to initiate a process of arbitration before I could get rid of this contractor and engage another one.

Nearly five years after inauguration, my house was ready for occupation. The other members of the family could not yet move in, for the younger generation's schools and colleges and my brothers' offices were all around Laxmipuram. So I kept my Yadavagiri house as a retreat for writing. I divided my time between Laxmipuram and Yadavagiri, enjoying the company of the family in one and of my books and papers in the other.

I had designed a small study – a bay-room with eight windows affording me a view in every direction: the Chamundi Hill temple on the south, a variety of spires, turrets, and domes on the east, sheep and cows grazing in the meadows on all sides, railway trains cutting across the east–west slope. I had a neighbour in the next compound, and a hint of another one half a mile away on rising ground in the west, where occasionally one could see a light at the window. I listened to the deep call of the woodcock in the still afternoons, and the cries of a variety of birds perching on the frangipani tree. Such perfection of surroundings, as I had already realized in my college days, was not conducive to study or writing. I spent long hours absorbed in the spectacle around and found it difficult to pull my thoughts back to writing. Subsequently I found it helpful to curtain off a large window beside my desk so that my eyes might fall on nothing more attractive than a grey drape, and thus I managed to write a thousand words a day and complete two novels and a number of short stories during the years of my isolation at Yadavagiri.

FOURTEEN

IN FEBRUARY 1956 my daughter married her cousin Chandru. In spite of house-building, I had put by enough to celebrate the wedding with music, feasting, lights, and the entertaining of a lot of guests assembled from all over south India, nor did I overlook the orthodox rites and rituals enjoined in the Scriptures.

When my daughter packed up and went away to live with her husband, I felt rather at a loose end at first. Having practised the role of a protective father all along, I found myself unemployed, but soon enjoyed the added rank of being a father-in-law. Both of them wrote to me regularly and the tone of their letters was full of assurance and confidence in their future. I realized they were a very happy couple.

This was the correct moment for the Rockefeller Foundation to think of me for a travel grant. I accepted the proposal and was lost during the following weeks in a set of unaccustomed activities such as passport-getting, inoculations, obtaining a bank permit, and form-filling – repeating any number of times my 'name in full,' 'father's name,' 'date of birth,' and so on. Finally I did break out of the triangular boundary of Madras, Mysore, and Coimbatore and left for the United States, in October 1956.

At this time I had been thinking of a subject for a novel: a novel about someone suffering enforced sainthood. A recent situation in Mysore offered a setting for such a story. A severe drought had dried up all the rivers and tanks; Krishnaraja Sagar, an enormous reservoir feeding channels that irrigated thousands of acres, had also become dry, and its bed, a hundred and fifty feet deep, was now exposed to the sky with fissures and cracks, revealing an ancient submerged temple, coconut stumps, and dehydrated crocodiles. As a desperate measure, the municipal council organized a prayer for rains. A group of Brahmins stood knee-deep in water (procured at great cost) on the dry bed of Kaveri, fasted, prayed, and chanted certain mantras continuously for eleven days. On the twelfth day it rained, and brought relief to the countryside.

This was really the starting point of *The Guide*. During my travels in America, the idea crystallized in my mind. I stopped in Berkeley for three months, took a hotel room, and wrote my novel. I shall quote from a journal I kept at that time:

BERKELEY

Another day of house-hunting, having firmly decided to stay in Berkeley rather than at Palo Alto in order to write my novel. Scrutinizing of advertisements in Berkeley *Gazetteer*, following up hearsay accounts of apartments available; thanks to Ed Harper's help visit the university housing centre, and tell one Mrs. Keyhoe (I could not concentrate on business, as my inner being clamoured to know if 'Key-hole' was being mis-spelt.) of my quest. 'Here is a man who wants a room for writing with kitchen facilities, private bath, prepared to pay et cetera, et cetera,' she would pour forth into a telephone. Finally we march out with a list in our hands . . . None of the apartments we inspect proves acceptable. While browsing around the campus bookstore on Telegraph, I suddenly look up and notice Hotel Carlton staring me in the face, never having noticed its presence before. Walk in and find Kaplan, the manager, extremely courteous and full of helpful suggestions – he's willing to give me a room where I may use a hot-plate for cooking my food, daily room service, separate bed and study, ideal in every way, the perfect hotel for me. And it costs seventy-five dollars a month.

Check out of my seven-dollar-a-day hotel at two and check in at Carlton at five minutes past two next afternoon. That very night acquire an electric hot-plate, a saucepan, rice, and vegetables, and venture to cook a dinner for myself. Profound relief that I don't have to face again the cafeteria carrot and tomato!

For the first time a settled place where I don't have to keep my possessions in a state of semi-pack. I am able to plan my work better. I am enchanted with the place, everything is nearby, two cinemas, three or four groceries, and any number of other shops; I can walk down and buy whatever I may need, and peep at the campanile clock to know the time; its chime is enchanting . . .

Nothing much to record, the same routine. I have got into the routine of writing – about one thousand five hundred to two thousand words a day anyhow. I have the whole picture ready in my mind, except for some detail here and there and the only question is to put it in writing. Some days when I feel I have been wasting time, I save my conscience by telling Kaplan at the desk, 'I am going to be very busy for the next few weeks trying to get on with my book.' A restatement of purpose is very helpful under these circumstances. Graham Greene liked the story when I narrated it to him in London. While I was hesitating whether to leave my hero alive or dead at the end of the story, Graham was definite that he should die. So I have on my hands the life of a man condemned to death before he was born and grown, and I have to plan my narrative to lead to it. This becomes a major obsession with me. I think of elaborate calculations: a thousand words a day and by February 1 I should complete the first draft. In order to facilitate my work I take a typewriter on hire; after three days of tapping away it gets on my nerves, and I lounge on the sofa and write by hand with my pen. Whatever the method, my mind has no peace unless I have written at the end of the day nearly two thousand words. Between breakfast and lunch I manage five hundred words, and while the rice on the stove is cooking, a couple of hundred, and after lunch once again till six, with interruptions to read letters and reply to them, or to go out for a walk along the mountain path, or meet and talk to one or the other of my many friends here . . .

Having written the last sentence of my novel, I plan to idle around Berkeley for a week and then leave on my onward journey. I have lived under the illusion that I would never have to leave Berkeley. All the friends I have in the world seem to be gathered there. Berkeley days were days of writing, thinking, and walking along mountain paths, and meeting friends. And so, when the time comes for me to plan to leave, I feel sad. How can I survive without a view of the Sather Gate Bookshop, the chime of the campanile clock, the ever-hurrying boys and girls in the street below, the grocer, the laundry, and the antique shop? I shall miss all these musical names on the streets – Dwight Way, Channing, Acton, Prospect, Piedmont, Shasta, Olympus, Sacramento – I shall miss all those scores of friends I have somehow managed to gather. I shall miss Lyla's voice on the telephone. When the sun shone the telephone was certain to ring and she would say, 'Isn't it a beautiful day?' . . .

The whole of Sunday busy cancelling my original plan to leave on Monday. The whole of Monday spent at bank counters, the baggage-forwarding agency, and the telegraph office. Late in the evening Biligiri dropped in. John came to ask if he could drive me to the airport next day, but the Vincents have

FIFTEEN

THE GUIDE attained a certain degree of popularity, which, though pleasant in itself, brought in its wake involvements that turned out to be ludicrous and even tragic.

In September 1964, Dev Anand, a film producer and actor of Bombay, wrote to me from New York and then arrived one morning at my Yadavagiri home with the single aim of acquiring *The Guide* for a film production.

A small crowd of autograph-seekers had gathered at my gate, while inside, in my drawing-room, after formal greetings and courtesies, Dev Anand took out his cheque-book, unscrewed the cap of his pen, and poised it over a cheque, waiting for me to pronounce my price for *The Guide*. He would draw any figure I might specify. This was too much for me. My thought processes became paralysed at the prospect of this windfall. I waved off his offer, held back his hand from inscribing more than a modest, reckonable advance against a small percentage on the future profits of the film.

I declared grandly, 'Let me rise or sink with your film. I do not want to exploit you.'

'With your co-operation, we will definitely go ahead; and then the sky will be the limit,' he said.

As we proceeded, the sky seemed to be lowered steadily, and when the time came to demand a share of the profits, you could puncture their sky with an umbrella. I was told finally that the film of *The Guide* had failed to make any profit. They wrote to me, 'We wish to assure you, however, that the moment we make any profit, your share will come to you automatically . . .' And there I have left it for seven years now. The picture was supposed to have cost them nearly ten million rupees, but much of it was spent on themselves, in fabulous salaries and princely living while producing the film. Now and then they summoned me for vague consultations or to participate in a meet-the-press party, where they proclaimed their grand intentions and achievements after benumbing their guests with free-flowing alcohol.

Once I was summoned to Bombay to dine with Lord Mountbatten at Government House and to persuade him to persuade Queen Elizabeth to attend the world première of *The Guide* in London. I was taken directly from the airport to the banquet hall at Government House. It was a fantastic proposal – which perhaps originated in the imagination of the late Pearl Buck, who was a partner of Dev Anand in the production of *The Guide*. After a regal banquet, our hostess, who was the Governor of Bombay, discreetly isolated the film unit from the other guests and piloted them to the presence of His Lordship, seated in a side veranda. We settled around with our lines ready. Lord Mountbatten suddenly asked, 'What's the story of *The Guide*?' Pearl Buck began to narrate it, but could not proceed very far with it. I heard her say, 'There was a man called Raju – he was a guide –'

'What guide?' asked His Lordship, in his deep voice.

This question upset her flow of narration. She turned to me and said, 'Narayan, you tell the story.'

I would not open my mouth. Dammit, I had taken eighty thousand words to tell the story; I was not going to be drawn into it now. Press announcements had given Pearl Buck credit for writing the screenplay, and it was said that she had been paid an advance of twenty-five or two hundred thousand dollars, and I was not going to help her out now. She looked pleadingly at me, and everyone there tried to egg me on. I sat tight. Pearl Buck meandered: 'There was Rosie – the dancer . . .'

'Oh!' exclaimed M. 'Who is she? What happened to her?' he asked with a sudden interest, which made Pearl Buck once again lose track of her own narration. I must admit that I enjoyed her predicament, as she treated Mountbatten to a mixed-up, bewildering version of *The Guide*. Other guests started to leave their distant posts and to infiltrate our carefully isolated group. 'Most interesting, I must say,' Lord Mountbatten now said. He turned to his aide. 'William, remind me when we get back to London. I don't know if the Queen will be free . . . However, I'll see what I can do.' A person who as a viceroy had handled the colossal task of transferring power from Britain to India in 1947, now to be expected to promote *The Guide* – it seemed absurd. However, nothing was heard of this proposal again.

*

The American director suddenly clamoured to have a scene where two tigers would fight for a deer and kill each other. The producer grumbled that it was unpractical and expensive. But the director, claiming his artistic heritage from Elia Kazan, explained, 'It will be symbolic. Also, being in colour the splash of blood on the screen will bring us rave notices, and then the sky will be the limit.' The catchphrase did the trick; Dev Anand accepted the proposal, and filmed a tiger-fight at Madras. But after editing, the sequence lasted half a second on the screen, and looked like a blob of colour left on carelessly at the processing laboratory, despite the blood-curdling roars and other sound effects.

At the beginning, before starting the picture, they went to

great trouble to seek my advice, and I had spent a whole day taking them round Mysore to show the riverside, forest, village, and crowds, granite steps and the crumbling walls of an ancient shrine which combined to make up the Malgudi of my story; they went away promising to return later with crew and equipment, but never came back. I learnt subsequently that they had shifted the venue of *The Guide* to Jaipur and had already shot several scenes on a location as distant from Malgudi as perhaps Iceland. When I protested, they declared, 'Where is Malgudi, anyway? There is no such place; it is abolished from this moment. For wide-screen purposes, and that in colour, Jaipur offers an ideal background; we can't waste our resources.'

By abolishing Malgudi, they had discarded my own values in milieu and human characteristics. My characters were simple enough to lend themselves for observation; they had definite outlines – not blurred by urban speed, size, and tempo. I did not expect the heroine, the dancer, to be more than a local star, but the film heroine became a national figure whose engagements caused her to travel up and down hundreds of miles each day in a Boeing 707, autographing, posing for photographers, emerging from five-star hotels and palatial neon-lit theatres. They had built her up into a V.I.P., so that her visit by plane and jeep to her dying lover was organized by the Defence Department at Delhi, thus glamourizing the death scene itself. The most outrageous part of it was the last scene, in which an elaborate funeral and prolonged lamentation were added at short notice in order to placate eleven financiers who saw the final copy of the film tightly clutching the money-bags on their laps, and who would not part with cash unless a satisfactory mourning scene was added.

Next, I had trouble with a stage adaptation of *The Guide* by an old friend of mine, Harvey Breit, who was at one time the literary editor of the *New York Times*. His version was so different from mine that I withheld my permission to present it on the stage. For instance, his version managed to abolish the heroine. I objected to his omission and to the addition of two irrelevant characters of his own; above all I objected to the hero's turning round and urinating on the stage. This controversy damaged our friendship to such an extent that at one point we had to communicate with each other only through lawyers. One morning in the year 1965, my lawyer telephoned me at the Chelsea Hotel in New York. 'R.K., listen! If you have no particular business to keep you here, leave New York immediately, or better still, leave the country. Harvey Breit is subpoenaing you for an arbitration. I've told his lawyer that I don't know your whereabouts. Quit before they discover you at the Chelsea . . . Yes, at once, immediately. If you are seen and the process-server drops the summons on the ground in front of you, you'll be committed. If you disobey it, you will be liable for contempt proceedings, which will be unpleasant. You will not be allowed to leave this country for six months or even a year.'

This was a terrifying prospect. I would not be able to maintain myself in New York for six months, or afford the legal expenses. I bundled up my belongings within an hour, spent a good part of the day cruising about in a taxi in the streets of New York (the best way to be lost to the world) and then, thanks to my friend Natwar Singh of our Foreign Service, secured asylum in the Indian Consulate until I could leave for the airport in the evening. I felt like a criminal on the run, a fugitive from a chain-gang. I remained in acute suspense until the Air India plane took off, afraid lest I should be off-loaded at the last minute to answer the summons. The summons, however, reached me in a plain cover, two weeks later, at Coimbatore. Ultimately, the arbitration did take place, and the verdict was in my favour.

The matter did not end there, however; Harvey Breit was too

SIXTEEN

OF ALL MY non-literary interests, 'arm-chair' agriculture, I find, has been most absorbing. I cut out and file country notes from newspapers, listen to the Farm Programme on the radio. I know how to get rid of weeds and pests, how to grow rice in flower pots, how to grow tomatoes without soil, the input proportion of fertilizer for such special tasks. I listen admiringly to any and every claim by a practical horticulturist as to how he manages to raise half a million flowers, jasmine or chrysanthemum, on a single acre, and despatch them to distant markets by air. I never doubt a word of whatever such an expert may say.

I sometimes speculated that if I possessed land, I'd be out at five in the morning in the field, with the early birds, and take a hand at ploughing, transplanting, weeding, and harvesting. The scent of earth and hay and the winnowed grains would be enough diversions for me. My afternoons would be spent in the flower garden. After watching the sunset, I would retire, following absolutely the plan and rhythm of Nature, a life uncomplicated by commerce or rush of any kind. This was perhaps the result of reading Thoreau's *Walden* and similar literature.

Driven by such recurring visions of 'back to the soil,' I secured, a couple of years ago, an acre of land in Bangalore, nearly a hundred miles from where I live. It was situated outside the city but within the municipal limits and housing projects of Bangalore, on the highway between Bangalore and Mysore. My acre was part of a hillock, and I had a whole rock, a mini-mountain, on my northern boundary. From its apex, my land went down in a gentle slope on to level ground. I had enough space to think of a split-level cottage with a wide veranda (the main thing would be the veranda); one whole side of the mini-mountain could serve as a sheer backdrop for the cottage at different levels down to a garage in the basement. I must find the right architect to design it. Beyond my land was a village with less than a hundred houses, dominated by a double-storeyed house in which the headman lived. I had to call on this person the first thing because I had noticed manure heaps (belonging to him) dumped on my part of the land and also maize seedlings flourishing on my soil. This made me uneasy. I had to pay him a diplomatic visit, and explain how I had become the owner of the land and how I felt honoured to be his neighbour. I took care not to sound too aggressive since I knew that all troubles around land started thus, and developed into a regular faction with civil litigations carried on for years, leaving little time for anyone to raise even a blade of grass.

The headman promised to have the dumps removed in due course, explaining that 'the boys' must have been spilling manure and seeds around. I promised him in return that I hoped to build a little shrine on the topmost rock of my mini-mountain, gather the village children in its corridors on an evening and teach them reading and writing, and impart to them various lessons about the modern world. As I spoke I suddenly discovered a purpose in life. If every person who is educated adopted a little group and imparted to it whatever knowledge he possessed, the 500 million population of India could be transformed in five years. Alas, my own pattern of life has left little time to put any of this into practice yet.

I lived in Mysore and, after leaving an agricultural expert on the spot to clear the land of stones and weeds and make it fit for cultivation, motored down off and on to watch his progress. He was a practical man, who knew all about soils and seeds and seasons. In due course my own maize plants stood four feet high, and I felt triumphant at the sight of them, but the field also teemed with trespassers. A well-worn foot-track cut diagonally across my land, connecting the highway with the villages beyond, and had been used by villagers from time immemorial. I had fenced my property with barbed wire strung across granite pillars but it did not affect the hoary practice; people just moved off a couple of pillars and pressed down the barbed wire, and there you were – the ancient passage continued. My agricultural expert explained that they weren't trespassers, but only rural folk passing from south to north as they had been doing for centuries.

'They won't disturb anything,' said the man casually.

'We must see when the corn ripens on the stalk,' I said full of misgivings. I did not like so much pedestrian traffic amidst my corn.

'We should put an end to it gradually, otherwise, we are likely to embitter the public,' he said. I began to have a feeling that I was the real intruder here. While passage for others was so well established, I soon discovered that I'd no legal access to my own plot. I myself had to trespass to reach it, over another man's ground. The man who had dumped manure on my ground owned all the land encircling mine! And he'd have no special reason to let me continue the use of the passage. My car had to be parked half a mile away on a stony track and I had to cross on foot through the man's land, and he could always, if he pleased, refuse me passage. I began to feel anxious about various little matters connected with the land.

Apart from all this, the economics of agriculture at first baffled me. Here was a world of completely inverted economic motives,

173

as it seemed, where you spent more money and willingly obtained less in return. This fact was realized by me when the harvest was brought to me at the end of the year's operations. During one of my periodic visits to my land, a bag was brought in and placed in the luggage boot of my car, a gunny sack half-filled with corn, garnered, salvaged, and sifted laboriously. When I reached home in Mysore and took it out proudly, I realized that its value in terms of money was about fifteen rupees. Eventually, when the accounts were to be settled, I had to meet a bill for four hundred and fifty rupees. When I asked my man, he explained, 'Labour, the watchman, and the levelling of the ground – we can't prepare the whole acre in a year, we'll do it little by little, and that is a capital investment. In course of time, it'll turn profitable.' The following year, it was the same story. A few further square yards of the ground were cleared of pebbles and levelled. I again got a half sackful of grain for nearly five hundred rupees. In the third year, there was nothing, as the rains had completely failed and all plants had wilted away to the roots. But the gradual levelling and clearing was still conducted, unaffected by considerations of debits and credits. I felt it might be cheaper to buy my needs in the market, but that is a wrong, and even irreverent, line of thinking. Agricultural operations have to be conducted in a spirit of give-and-take, in the teeth of hostile forces engendered by men, seasons, and pests, which must be overcome with non-violence and faith in one's ultimate victory. The hustle of city life will not work in this area. Like the corn, agricultural problems must also be allowed to have their stages of rawness, ripeness, and withering away!

SEVENTEEN

I AM INCLINED to call this the last chapter, but how can an autobiography have a final chapter? At best it can only be a penultimate one; nor can it be given a rounded-off conclusion, as is possible in a work of fiction. The ending in a book of this sort must necessarily be arbitrary and abrupt.

I would like to dwell for a little while in the present tense, but I realize that it may turn out to be rambling and fragmentary, as I try to compress the contemporary experience into a neat framework. The past, even the recent past, has an advantage of falling into well-defined boundaries, but the present constantly boils over and flows out in all directions.

After remaining out of sight for many years, an old friend turned up at my house recently. He was an authority in economics, who had served in various academic and industrial bodies for three decades. I found him, though my contemporary, relatively more aged. He used to be a cheerful, lively person even in his fifties. But now I found that he was preoccupied with cholesterol, blood-pressure, and diabetes. He hesitated to accept any food or drink. No doctor had ever advised him to keep off this or that, but he imposed restrictions on himself after acquiring a lot of unwarranted medical information. He enquired how I felt about my health. When I answered, rather lightheartedly, that I was not giving it any thought yet, he looked disappointed, as if without cholesterol et cetera there was no common ground between us. I changed the subject, but I realized that whatever the subject, he liked to worry about it. He said, 'After thirty years of active public service, won't you agree that I am entitled to peace of mind?'

'What's spoiling it?'

He looked puzzled and said, 'I don't know – I rebuilt my house so that my daughter and son-in-law may live in comfort and also nearby, but you know it is very painful every morning to watch the girl bully her child to start for the school, and later about homework – it's all painful.' He paused to consider what other irritations he might think of, and added, 'And then my wife. Her shopping habit! When she goes into the market, it is hours before she can be seen again; and I sit in the car moping! If I engage a driver I know he will ruin the car. But where can one find a good driver nowadays?'

At my age, encountering a contemporary is like looking into a mirror. After he left, I questioned myself, 'Am I entitled to peace of mind or not? How much of it do I possess or deserve?' If I have to worry, it's about things outside me, mostly not concerning me. I generally fret about municipal shortcomings; when I find the streets not properly lit, I bother the officials with telephone calls and letters. Every minute I find myself on the point of dashing off virulent letters to newspapers about corruption and inefficiency that may come to my notice. I have also taken upon myself the impossible task of protecting the thousands of trees of Mysore, and constantly appeal to the civic authorities to save them from goatherds and roadside vandals. The frangipani in front of my house, grown taller and wider than ever, is a perennial concern for me. For four months from October on, it sheds its leaves and produces thousands of pale yellow flowers, pleasingly charging the air with their perfume day and night. It attracts swarms of men, women, and children from the surrounding villages, who collect the flowers for the goddess in a little shrine at the Palace Port. I have to keep appealing across our fence, 'Shake down the flowers, don't snap the branches.' One of my major preoccupations today is how to save the Kukanahalli Tank, which meant so much to me in the days of my 'Divine Music.' The tank's surface is shrinking alarmingly, with water hyacinth sucking off all the moisture. And no one seems to care!

After the morning coffee, I sit for a while in the veranda chair to discuss with my brother the state of the nation and of the world in general, after a perusal of the headlines in the morning paper which usually provokes gloomy speculations of all sorts – political, economic, and others, at the start of the day. Sometimes we discuss ways of mitigating disasters, or we take heart from an ancient mythological episode in which an all-powerful demon abducted the Earth and hid it in the bed of some Cosmic Ocean, and an *avatar* of Vishnu dug it out and set it on its course again, after destroying the demon. So there is hope. Or gradually we might also lose sight of the problems of survival in watching birds alight on a twisted log of teak* mounted upright amidst our crotons. A basin of water is kept at the base of the pillar, and most birds take a dip before flying off. The woodpecker, the woodcock, and the black warbler, which were noticeable when I was just building this house, are all still here, or their progeny perhaps; they live in the trees at the back yard – the mango, breadfruit, and 'rose'-berry, little saplings planted years ago, with hardly any hope that they would grow into a wood.

*

* A pure freak from the forests, where some primeval hurricane, sweeping through, seems to have lashed together as in an irrevocable deadlock or wedlock two neighbouring teakwood saplings and left them to grow up spirally.

Accumulation of paper is a palpable token of one's career, I suppose. In my four decades of writing a mountainous quantity of paper has accumulated around me – manuscripts at various stages, letters, documents, photographs, and mementoes, and the thought of it fills me with despair. I burn great piles of them from time to time, including manuscripts, but yet their level keeps rising in a black cabin trunk in which all papers are generally dumped. I am constantly planning to organize or destroy them once for all – but at the moment, I feel that I should let others decide their fate. My publisher and friend, Marshall Best, when he visited me in Mysore years ago, watched me while I searched for an important note, and suggested that I needed a curator rather than a secretary. It was a welcome hint.

My life has fallen firmly into a professional pattern: books, agents, contracts, and plenty of letter-writing to known and unknown persons alike, and, of course, travel over and over again. But my personal life has become more interesting. Although my main address is in Mysore, I find every excuse to drive a hundred and twenty miles over a mountain road to visit my daughter and spend an unspecified number of days in her company; there I have a comfortable room for my use where I can sleep, study, or write undisturbed, and also enjoy my grandchildren's company. My granddaughter would resent being called a grandchild now. When I was writing *The Man-Eater of Malgudi*, she was at the stage of squeezing herself beside me in my chair and carrying on an undertone conversation with her doll all the time I was writing; but today she is a high-school girl (till recently), interested in Enid Blyton, film music over the radio, and Malgudi tales. Some months ago, she set up a model of Malgudi, with miniature streets and buildings, during the Navarathri festival of dolls; she helps me nowadays by taking dictation and typing my letters. My grandson is eleven years old, an exact copy of Swami in *Swami and Friends*, at the same stage I was in if you turn back in this book to pages 45–46. He is a very busy grandson, totally absorbed in his school politics, homework, cricket team, cycling, and ping-pong. Whenever he feels he is neglecting art, he picks up his bamboo flute and practises music or plays on his drum. Three years ago, when he was convalescing after an appendix operation, he was interested in writing. I lent him my portable typewriter, and he sat up in bed and typed away all day with two fingers. Sometimes he copied from a storybook, and sometimes spun out an original story. One such was called 'Grand' (he would not explain why), and I give it below:

'Once upon a time there was a man and his father. They were so poor. No one to help them. One day his father's birthday came. Then that man became very rich. Then his son became poor. Then another day his uncle came. His father's son's birthday came. Then his uncle became so rich. Give me the monies, said the man. Then the uncle became so poor. Then his father told uncle, Go to R. K. Narayan and take some monies. Then he will be so poor.'

I liked the story for the ease with which it conveys in one sweep the complexities, muddles, and demands of kinship, and the ups and downs of man's fortunes – enough substance to fill a novel; above all my name involved in it afforded me a refreshingly objective view of myself. Recently I confronted my grandson with his composition. (Not easy to get his attention nowadays even for a few minutes, but I caught him in the passage as he came in from school and before he could run out to play.) He glanced through it indifferently and shook his head disapprovingly: 'I wrote it so long ago! I was young then. Throw it away, please.' I explained that I couldn't. He remained thoughtful for a moment, and said, 'That uncle is not a real uncle, but only a next-house man. They all spent their monies too much on birthday parties, buying